SUN SEA & SOLIDARITY

21 YEARS OF BRISTOL'S LINK WITH BEIRA

BY SUSIE WELDON

BITA

BRISTOL CITY COUNCIL

BRISTOL LINK WITH BEIRA

UWE BRISTOL

University of the West of England

⊘ Tangent Books

First published 2012 by Tangent Books
in partnership with Bristol International Twinnings Association
Tangent Books
Unit 5.16 Paintworks
Bristol BS4 3EH

0117 972 0645
www.tangentbooks.co.uk

Publisher: Richard Jones
Richard@tangentbooks.co.uk

ISBN 9781906477677

Copyright: Southern Africa Resource Centre
(operating as Bristol Link with Beira)
www.bristolbeiralink.org

Design: Joe Burt
(joe@wildsparkdesign.com)

Print management: Jonathan Lewis
(essentialprintmanagement@gmail.com)

The BLB would like to thank UWE for their kind sponsorship, Richard
Jones and Tangent Books for their patient support, Susie Weldon for
doing such a thorough and amazing job, Alix Hughes and BITA for
providing contacts and the original idea, and Forward Maisokwadzo
for his journalistic experience and fundraising skills.

A CIP record for this book is available from the British Library

Printed in the UK using paper from a sustainable source.

CONTENTS

06 INTRODUCTION

08 ABOUT MOZAMBIQUE

14 ABOUT BEIRA

20 HISTORY OF BLB

38 HEALTH

48 WOMEN

56 EDUCATION

62 CULTURE

68 LIFE

72 THE NEXT 20 YEARS

74 MOZAMBIQUE TIMELINE

79 LINKS

TO THE PEOPLE OF
BRISTOL AND BEIRA

FOREWORD

I have great pleasure in congratulating Bristol Link with Beira on *Sun, Sea & Solidarity*, the story of 21 years of friendship and solidarity between the citizens of Bristol and Beira. The title is particularly apt. Mozambique would not have been able to achieve peace and security without international solidarity – particularly the solidarity of the British people – which went beyond the support for the war for independence, and continues to this day in its many manifestations.

As High Commissioner of the Republic of Mozambique in the United Kingdom for nearly 10 years from 2002, I had the unique privilege of witnessing the blossoming of this special relationship that has brought tangible benefits to the peoples of both cities and countries. I would like to pay tribute to the pioneers of this visionary enterprise celebrated in *Sun, Sea & Solidarity*, and to those who worked tirelessly in the past two decades to preserve and strengthen the bonds of this friendship.

It is worth recalling that this twinning materialised at a time when Mozambique was still embroiled in a bloody conflict that raged for 16 long years and killed, maimed and displaced millions of people, before peace was eventually achieved in October 1992. The twinning was not only a gesture of solidarity of the highest standing, but it also carried with it an intrinsic message of hope and encouragement that there were people in places such as Bristol who cared about the plight of the Mozambican people and were prepared to extend a hand of friendship in their hour of need.

The relationship has navigated the historical paths in both countries over the last 21 years and endured precisely because it is inspired by a genuine desire to work together and make a difference. This book is an eloquent tribute to the benefits of people-to-people solidarity and cooperation.

Long live the friendship between Bristol and Beira!

His Excellency Antonio Gumende, Ambassador and Permanent Representative of Mozambique to the United Nations.

INTRODUCTION

BY PAUL DUNN

Paul Dunn has been involved with Bristol Link with Beira from its earliest days and was chair for many years until he retired in 2011. He reflects on the charity's work over the last two decades

In certain ways, it hardly seems possible that we have managed to clock up more than 20 years of linking work with our friends in Beira. I say that because there have been a few people who have been Trustees throughout that period and they have stayed the course. This book provides the opportunity to share some of the developments and achievements that we have delivered together.

All the main twinning associations in Bristol try to mark significant anniversaries in a tangible way. This book is our way of sharing our enthusiasm for internationalism, solidarity and development and we would like to send a huge "muito obrigado" to the University of the West of England's Better Together Fund for the grant to make it a reality.

We are very fortunate to have the support of a (relatively) new tranche of Trustees, including the chair, Peninah Achieng. These Trustees have provided new energy and ideas. What this book can help with is an organisational memory of why we set up Bristol Link with Beira (BLB) and what our motivations have been for over two decades.

In terms of our achievements, the most important has been to keep in touch with Beira City Council for so long, when communication has often been difficult. Remember that Mozambique is still one of the poorest countries in the world and Beira does not have much capacity for maintaining their part of the link with Bristol. That

they have, shows how much they appreciate two-way contact with us. Of course, there are other people who have helped to sustain this relationship: for example, the part-time workers we have in Bristol and Beira; BITA coordinator; UK High Commissioners in Maputo; Mozambican High Commissioners in London; Mayors of Beira; teachers in schools; and people working on our many projects.

Our link has always been about people. We were sure at the start of this journey that we wanted to bring people together across our continents, notwithstanding the huge distance that separates us, and our use of different languages.

People around the world have always lived in uncertain times and that is true for us all today. Of course, despite the cuts being imposed on public spending in the UK currently, the UK is still a rich country. What we have found over the years, is that wealth is not just about money, but is also about friendship, solidarity, honesty, history, culture, sport, music, art, enthusiasm and a sense of international comradeship.

It is difficult to predict what might happen in the next year, let alone the next 20 years. But, with continued passion and hard work, there is every reason to believe that our wonderful link with the people of Beira will continue to thrive. After all, helping to bring the people of the world a little step closer has rarely been more important.

ABOUT MOZAMBIQUE

"Madness does not govern a country; discussion does"
Mozambican proverb

MOZAMBIQUE'S SO-CALLED 'CIVIL WAR' (1977-1992)

For much of the last century, Mozambique's history has been written in blood. After 500 years of repression under Portuguese colonial rule, the battle for independence started in the 1960s as a guerrilla campaign by Frelimo (Frente de Libertação de Moçambique).

This came to an abrupt end after Portugal's fascist regime was overturned at home by a leftist military coup and power handed to Frelimo in 1975. However, the new government had no time to enjoy its independence because within a couple of years, a new and more brutal war had begun.

The military campaign that followed independence and caused so much suffering is often called the Mozambique Civil War although in fact it was funded, engineered and propagated to a very large extent by external forces; first Rhodesia (today Zimbabwe) and then South Africa. This was an externally perpetrated war to destabilise the new Mozambican state and deny a refuge to southern Africa's liberation movements, especially South Africa's African National Congress (ANC). This is how it unfolded:

1975 Following Mozambique's independence, tensions rise among its white minority-ruled neighbours after the new Government allows two black resistance movements – South Africa's ANC and Rhodesia's ZANU – to operate from inside the country. At the same time, Western allies fear a communist take-over in southern Africa; with friends in the Soviet Union, Cuba and China, newly independent Mozambique is seen as a tinderbox waiting to explode.

1976 To counter this, Rhodesia, and later South Africa, fund an opposition movement, the Mozambique National Resistance Movement (Renamo).

1977 Renamo begins a violent guerrilla war against the ruling Frelimo party, kidnapping civilians, including children, and forcing them to fight.

1980-1992 After Rhodesia's independence in 1980, South Africa becomes Renamo's main supporter. South Africa wages a covert war against Mozambique through Renamo, which it finances and arms, and also through raids by its own commandos, with devastating impacts both on civilians and the country's economy.

The Mozambique Civil War is cruel, bloody and brutal and atrocities are committed on both sides. However, refugees interviewed for a

1988 report by US-State Department consultant Robert Gersony attribute 94% of the murders and abductions and 93% of the lootings to Renamo.

Renamo tactics include mass killing, rape and mutilation of civilians, child soldiers and forced labour. Health workers are kidnapped and killed, bus passengers are clubbed to death, shops are burned and villages destroyed, and vital infrastructure such as railway lines and bridges are bombed.

In 1987 a Canadian fact-finding mission visited Mozambique. It reported: "We found a situation in which almost four of the 14 million children and women and men populating Mozambique are in imminent danger of starvation – a tragedy of Ethiopian proportions. We found more than 42% of the population on the move, forced to abandon fields and homes by the massive bandit (Renamo) activities throughout the rural areas."

Renamo will later be described in the United Nations as guilty of "one of the most brutal holocausts against ordinary human beings since World War II".

1992 According to a 1992 UN report, humans are the most endangered species in Mozambique. This is the year, however, in which fighting ends after, wearied by the bloodshed, Frelimo and Renamo sign a peace accord.

The Mozambican Civil War has lasted for 15 years and cost the lives of more than one million people in fighting and starvation, including an estimated 500,000 childhood deaths between 1981–88 alone.

Around six million are displaced, 1.7 million people have fled the country, and around one million landmines have been planted in the countryside. These will cause misery, injury and death for decades to come.

(For more on Mozambique's history, read the timeline on page 74) .

KILL EVERYTHING, STEAL EVERYTHING, BURN EVERYTHING

In 1984, President Samora Machel said of South Africa's war on Mozambique:

"Our people had their property looted, their houses destroyed, their granaries looted, their crops pillaged and flattened, their cattle stolen and killed, their tools burnt and destroyed.

"The communal villages and cooperatives, the schools and clinics, the wells and dams built by the people with so much effort and sacrifice became targets for the enemy's criminal fury…

"The systematic destruction of economic infrastructure, bridges and roads, shops and warehouses, sawmills, plantations, agricultural and industrial machinery, electricity supply lines, fuel tanks, lorries and buses, locomotives and carriages has prevented the implementation of economic development projects of the utmost importance for the wellbeing of the Mozambican people.

"The bandits have murdered and kidnapped peasants and members of cooperatives, parliamentary deputies and party militants, teachers and students, nurses, lorry drivers, engine drivers, agricultural, construction and commercial workers, technicians in various sectors, nuns, priests, private shopkeepers, journalists and civil servants...

"This is the enemy's cruel nature – kill everything, steal everything, burn everything…

"Only future generations will show the precise extent of the social trauma caused by the horrors and barbarity of the armed gangs. The children who witnessed atrocities and repugnant acts of violence and destruction will grow up with the nightmare of their tragic memories.

"Men and women have been permanently mutilated and maimed, both physically and psychologically. They will be living evidence of the cruelty of the war waged against us."

MOZAMBIQUE FAST FACTS

OFFICIAL NAME: Republic of Mozambique (República de Moçambique).

LOCATED: On the southeastern coast of Africa between Tanzania and South Africa. It shares borders with 6 countries and has a coastline that stretches along the Indian Ocean for more than 1,500 miles.

AREA: 308,642 sqare miles – roughly three times the size of the UK.

POPULATION: Around 23.4 million people, around half of which are children. Around 70% live in rural areas and make their living from agriculture.

ETHNIC GROUPS: Around 60 ethic groups, the biggest being the Makua-Lomwé who make up 37% of the population. The official language is Portuguese.

CLIMATE: Mozambique has a hot tropical climate. It is vulnerable to natural disasters such as floods, cyclones, earthquakes and droughts.

BRIEF HISTORY: A Portuguese colony for around 500 years, Mozambique gained its independence in 1975 but experienced a violent civil war from 1977 to 1992 that caused a million deaths and resulted in 1.7 million refugees. Mozambique has been at peace since then but has massive challenges thanks to the legacy of war, lack of development during colonial era and its vulnerability to natural disasters.

POVERTY LEVELS: Mozambique is one of the poorest countries in the world, ranked 184 out of 187 countries on the 2011 Human Development Index, which is compiled each year to measure standards of living across the world. The government is working hard to improve life for its citizens. The

estimated average life expectancy was only 42 years in 2000 but is now around 51 years for men and 52.5 years for women (compared to 77.9 and 82.5 respectively for the UK).

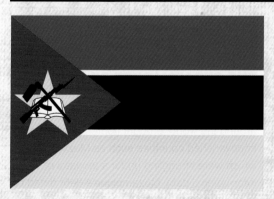

SYMBOLISM OF THE MOZAMBICAN FLAG

Green = the riches of the land
White = peace
Black = the African continent
Yellow = Mozambique's minerals
Red = the struggle for independence
Rifle = defence and vigilance
Hoe = agriculture
Open book = education
Star = Marxism and internationalism

MOZAMBIQUE TODAY

Mozambique was a Portuguese colony from the 16th century until it gained its independence in 1975 – only to plunge immediately into a bloody war funded, organised and perpetrated largely by outside forces. The war claimed the lives of over one million people in fighting and starvation and set back Mozambique's development by decades.

Today, 20 years after the war ended in 1992, Mozambique is at peace. The government has won praise for its efforts to implement a health system, improve education and boost the economy, which has grown fast over the last decade.

The so-called green zones on the urban fringe of Beira are below sea level and used to grow rice. Beaches are deserted and used by fishermen during the week but on Sundays are packed with families.

Mozambique has vast and untapped natural resources. It has held several free and peaceful elections since the end of the war although it is still dominated by one party, Frelimo. Its economy has been growing steadily, expanding by 6.6% in 2010, for example. In many ways Mozambique is seen as one of Africa's success stories.

ONE OF THE POOREST COUNTRIES IN THE WORLD

Yet Mozambique remains one of the poorest countries in the world thanks to the legacy of war, centuries of inequality under Portuguese rule and its vulnerability to natural disasters such as floods and droughts.

It is listed as 184 out of 187 countries on the 2011 Human Development Index – a measurement of quality of life, including life expectancy and standards of living, compiled every year by the United Nations Development Programme.

Around 75% of the population earns less than US$1.25 (about 78p) a day, with 54% described as being in absolute poverty. Most live in rural areas, surviving by subsistence farming. Annual floods and drought threaten food security and rural livelihoods.

Despite a growing economy, Mozambique relies heavily on foreign aid which makes up around a quarter of the national income and half of the state budget. No wonder Britain's High Commissioner to Mozambique Shaun Cleary described the country as a paradox: "A case of success yet still one of the poorest countries in the world".

THE STRAITJACKET OF DEBT

The 2000 floods, which made headlines around the world, brought home the plight of impoverished countries such as Mozambique, which were struggling under a tsunami of international debt. Mozambique's debt dated back to the mid-1970s when the newly independent nation was encouraged to borrow money to build clothing factories and to develop plantations to export cotton and bananas.

Then the civil war broke out, and trade ground to a halt while the country's infrastructure was destroyed. As interest on the original debt stacked up, Mozambique was lent more money to rebuild the nation – adding to its debt.

As Dr Joseph Hanlon of the Open University observed in 2005: "Mozambique is still paying the price – repaying loans that were given to help it feed people after South Africa destroyed farms and factories… Instead of rebuilding after the war, Mozambique had to concentrate on paying debts."

At the time of the flood, Mozambique owed US$6.4billion to international institutions. Charities and pressure groups, including Bristol's Southern Africa Resource Centre, campaigned for the debt

to be written off on the grounds that states such as Mozambique deserved real help in the face of disaster, rather than lending them more money to pay back more debt.

As Mozambican economist Carlos Castel-Branco told the BBC at the time: "We cannot pay our debt with water. The World Bank will not accept water. But that is all we have."

In December 2005, the IMF cancelled all Mozambican IMF debt contracted prior to January 1, 2005, worth U.S. $153 million, and in July 2006, the World Bank did the same for around $1.3 billion. Around a fifth of Mozambique's debt was written off, but nearly four fifths remain.

HOW MOZAMBIQUE COMPARES TO THE UK

Mozambique is three times bigger than the United Kingdom and has less than a seventh of our population. A quick look at the figures shows the glaring inequalities:

* Sources: United Nations, World Health Organisation & The World Factbook

MOZAMBIQUE

POPULATION: 22.3 million people (2011 estimate)
- 3% make it to old age (65+ years)
- 51% are children (under 15 years)

LIFE EXPECTANCY:
- 51 years for men
- 52.5 years for women

INFANT MORTALITY: 79 deaths/1000 live births

HIV/AIDS:
- 1.4 million people live with HIV/AIDS
- 74,000 deaths from AIDS
- HIV prevalence in adults: 11.5%

NUMBER OF DOCTORS: 3 per 100,000 population

UNITED KINGDOM

POPULATION: 62.6 million (2011 estimate)
- 16% make it to old age (65+ years)
- 19% are children (under 15 years)

LIFE EXPECTANCY:
- 77.9 years for men
- 82.5 years for women

INFANT MORTALITY: 0.12 deaths/1000 live births

HIV/AIDS:
- 85,000 people live with HIV/AIDS
- Fewer than 1,000 deaths from AIDS
- HIV prevalence in adults: 0.2%

NUMBER OF DOCTORS: 274 per 1,000 population*

ABOUT BEIRA

'There is no cockerel without a comb'
Mozambican proverb

CITY OF HOPE AND ASPIRATIONS

Beira is Mozambique's second biggest city and one of its most important ports. Located in Sofala Province, it was once a Muslim settlement and has been a centre of trade for centuries, thanks to its favoured position on the coast where the Pungue River pours into the Indian Ocean.

The Portuguese established Beira as an important base in the late 1800s. They built the port and railway that made Beira one of East Africa's most important trading cities in the 1900s, shipping minerals, tobacco, sugar, cotton and grain in and out of Central Africa.

Thanks to its booming economy, Beira was known as a bustling, cosmopolitan city, and its sandy beaches made it a popular holiday destination for white colonials. They perhaps didn't notice the shanty towns that circled the attractive Mediterranean-style squares and colonial villas of the city centre, where Beira's African inhabitants lived without basic water and sanitation facilities.

Like so much of Mozambique, Beira collapsed in the decades following independence in 1975. The white ethnic Portuguese and middle classes, who had dominated government and business, left en masse, and the devastating civil war that gripped Mozambique from 1977 to 1992 plunged the city into poverty, causing widespread famine and disease. The symbol of Beira's decline is the Grande Hotel. Once a luxurious hotel billed as the "pride of Africa", it became a refugee camp during the civil war and the structure, stripped of all fittings, is still occupied by thousands of squatter families today. The railway lines to Rhodesia and Malawi were repeatedly bombed during the civil war, with a huge impact upon trade. In his book *Beggar Your Neighbours: Apartheid Power in Southern Africa*, Dr Joseph Hanlon accuses South African commandos of deliberately targeting Beira to destabilise Mozambique's economy, bombing

BEIRA FAST FACTS

- Mozambique's second largest city
- Located in Sofala Province roughly halfway down Mozambique's coast
- Population of around 600,000 people
- Known for its steamed crab and prawn
- Major port and rail links to Central Africa, shipping goods such as cotton, cashews, prawns, sugarcane, tea, cassava and corn.
- The only Renamo-led administration in Frelimo-dominated Mozambique
- Devastated in the 2000 Mozambique flood

Clockwise from top left: Mussodji playing in Beira in 2008; the Grande Hotel, once luxurious, now occupied by thousands of squatter families; vegetable stall; Beira lighthouse.

key railway bridges, the oil pipeline and marker buoys in Beira port, for example.

Beira suffered again in the 2000 Mozambique flood that devastated the city and surrounding region, leaving millions homeless and severely damaging buildings, roads and industry.

BEIRA TODAY

Like the rest of Mozambique, Beira's problems are enormous. It has some charming Mediterranean-style houses and interesting sights, such as the Cathedral of Beira and the Fort of San Gaetano, but the legacy of the war years can be seen in its dilapidated buildings and roads, and in the poverty that is evident throughout the city.

As a report by the Industrial Development Corporation of South Africa, which visited Mozambique in September 2006, says: "Beira feels like it is operating on a quarter capacity – there's still a bustle to the markets and streets but there's also a distinct feel of jaded former glory with little sign of large scale commerce and street after street of empty shops."

Despite its many problems, the city is on the up again. It is growing fast – its population rose by over a quarter between the 1990s and 2000s

– and today numbers around 500,000, with 40% aged 15 or under, according to the 2007 census.

The local government – the first of only two Renamo-led administrations in the country – is trying to improve services. It is prioritising clearing drainage ditches to minimise flooding, providing clean water and sanitation and building new health centres. It's also trying to attract business investment to bring much-needed jobs and money to the city.

And the port is busy once again. Millions of tonnes of goods, from coal and aluminium are shipped through Beira every year, and the administration is seeking international assistance to deepen the harbour and improve the railway network to make Beira one of East Africa's most important shipping ports once again.

The Lord Mayor of Bristol Councillor Peter Abraham being presented with a flag by head of culture Paul Barnett on behalf of the executive mayor of Beira.

BEIRA CITY FLAG

Beira adopted a municipal flag in 2005. At its centre is an African shield showing the modern train station in front of a rising sun, as well as an anchor and harbour.

THE EXTRAORDINARY MAYOR OF BEIRA

Daviz Mbepo Simango is a remarkable man: an engineer by background and a Protestant (most Mozambicans are Catholic or Muslim), he heads only the second Renamo administration in a country where the old national anthem began: "Viva viva Frelimo" before being replaced with the less partisan "Patria Amada".

The son of a Frelimo politician, Simango became the Renamo mayor of Beira in 2003. He is popular in Beira, where he is seen as energetic, efficient and effective; he has won several awards for good leadership and governance. But after a row with party leaders, who de-selected Simango as the Renamo candidate in 2009, allegedly for not giving jobs to Renamo members,

he stood as an independent and, following a fraught campaign, won with 60% of the vote. He was expelled from Renamo and founded the Democratic Movement of Mozambique (MDM), with a cockerel as its symbol.

MDM then stood in Mozambique's 2009 presidential elections and came third with 8.6% of the vote to Frelimo's landslide 75%. That was a remarkable result considering MDM had been banned from fielding candidates in nine of the 13 parliamentary regions on the grounds that its registration papers were not in order.

Simango has survived one assassination attempt and is being touted as 'the new face of the opposition' in Mozambique. He is clearly a man to watch. He has developed a very good relationship with the Bristol Link with Beira.

A DAY IN THE LIFE...

In 2006 Angelinha, a pupil at Beira's First of May Pre-School, gave BLB volunteer Kevin Seely a glimpse into her life. Angelinha lives in Beira's vast Goto slum with her mother and sisters.

Heading home after school...

to one of Beira's poorest areas...

In the street outside my home...

At home with my mum...

Inside our house with my mum and baby sister...

Helping wash the dishes...

Preparing to fetch water...

Petting the family goat...

HISTORY OF BLB

"There are no shortcuts to the top of the palm tree"
Mozambican proverb

BRISTOL LINK WITH BEIRA: TWO DECADES OF SOLIDARITY AND FRIENDSHIP

Bristol signed a Friendship Agreement with Beira in Mozambique on December 11, 1990, at a formal event officiated by the Mozambique Ambassador, His Excellency Lieutenant Armando Panguene, and the Lord Mayor of Bristol, Councillor Jim Williams.

The idea was the initiative of the Bristol Anti-Apartheid Movement which was very active in the 1980s and wanted to reach out to one of Africa's most impoverished nations – one which had suffered in the battle against apartheid.

"Beira was chosen because Mozambique was one of the frontline states in the fight against apartheid," recalls Paul Dunn, who was involved with BLB from the beginning and chair of trustees until 2011.

"Mozambique was badly damaged by apartheid. The South Africa-backed war was still underway so twinning with Beira was seen as an act of solidarity with Mozambique. Also, Beira was a port city, like Bristol, with a similar population to Bristol."

BLB treasurer Steve Strong, who has also been involved with the Link with Beira from the start, says choosing Beira "wasn't a very scientific" process. "It was very simple, really: it was a port, of similar size to Bristol, and of significance to the economy of the country. And it began with a 'B'," he adds, only half joking.

First they had to find out if Beira would be interested. And that wasn't easy, recalls Bevis Miller, then chair of Bristol Anti-Apartheid Committee (the biggest in the country).

"I talked to the embassy in London and they said 'what a really good idea', and we waited and waited and got nothing back," he says. "So we started faxing the office of the governor in Beira and still nothing. So eventually I bit the bullet and went out there in 1989.

Children on the beach in Beira.

"In those days you used faxes and I faxed the office saying 'I'm coming'; no reply but miraculously there was a car and a driver waiting at the airport. I've never been so relieved!

"They looked after me very well, and showed me around and I met the council and outlined our ideas. I think they looked at me in disbelief and thought 'this is never going to happen' but we established a relationship and then it took off."

FACT-FINDING DELEGATION

In November 1989, a three-person delegation went out to Beira to look at how a twinning arrangement could work. They found a city devastated by the long years of war, in a country that the United Nations had assessed as the second most deprived nation in the world.

So appalling were conditions in Mozambique that three years later the UN would declare human beings to be the most endangered species in the country.

In Beira itself unemployment levels were around 70%. Most people scratched a living through selling goods on street corners. For those with a job, the average wage was around £15 per month (in the UK it was 76 times this amount).

The poverty was acute. "There was an absolutely dire need for resources; the Portuguese had smashed up so much when they left – tractors, engines, boats, equipment, etc," says Paul Dunn who was part of the delegation.

Only one in five residents were connected to the sewage system; many lived in shacks without running water or electricity in the city's sprawling slums.

The most sophisticated piece of equipment available to the head of administration for the city council – for a city approximately the size of Bristol, with 350,000 residents – was a manual typewriter.

The education system was struggling to cope with just 890 teachers for 46,700 pupils; classrooms were crammed with 70 or 80 pupils and schools operated three shifts, with the first starting at 6am. Despite this, around 13,000 pupils a year could not attend school at all because there was no room for them.

"Most schools didn't have concrete floors, qualified teachers, desks," recalls Paul. Escola Primaria Angostinho Neto school was typical. It had opened in 1948, had 24 teachers for 1,200 pupils and was, the delegation reported afterwards, "in poor physical shape".

The report added: "There is little glass in the windows and many of the classrooms have water on the floor. Floorboards are missing on the stage in the main hall. It is difficult to organise classes for so many children and they do not have enough desk and chairs."

South Africa's war of destabilisation was still going on; during one of its school visits the delegation came uncomfortably close to it, says Paul: "We heard machine guns – AK47s – going off in the direction we were about to go in. People were really nervous. They were still coming in from country areas to towns because they were safer in the city."

Despite the poverty and the very real hardships, Paul recalls "the warmth and openness of the people; they were very trusting" – and also the hope aroused by the delegation's visit: "Managing expectations was really difficult. We spent all our time saying 'we're a very small organisation'," he says.

The delegation returned to Bristol with ideas of what could be done. The Beira Fund was set up to raise money and a charity, Bristol-based Southern Africa Resource Centre, established to run it.

Bristol City Council supported the initiative from the start. It was enthusiastic about twinning, believing it helped foster a sense of global citizenship. It provided premises for SARC at a peppercorn rent and the Lord Mayor of Bristol Jim Williams (by coincidence Bristol's first black Lord Mayor) officiated alongside Mozambique Ambassador Armando Panguene at the opening.

The council also provided twinning co-ordinator

support through Bristol International Twinnings Association (BITA) as well as small grants and venues for events, and the University of the West of England also gave logistical support to the BITA coordinator.

From the beginning the aim was to provide practical help, focusing on health and education projects with an emphasis on listening to what local people said they needed. "Genuinely our primary interest was to be connected to local people enough to understand what would be most useful to them and we were guided a lot by that as well as the practicalities of what was possible," says Steve.

CONTAINERS OF AID

One of the newly formed Link's first activities was to send a 20ft container of clothes, medicines, school materials and office equipment to Beira. The container was sponsored by a wide range of organisations: Bristol City Council, Avon County Council, Christian Aid, the World Development Movement, War on Want, Traidcraft, Bristol Trades Union Congress (TUC), South West Regional TUC, Bristol Mozambique-Angola Campaign, Bristol Anti-Apartheid Movement and National Union of Teachers' Avon division.
Loaded at Avonmouth and shipped to Mozambique, it also contained sewing machines,

Volunteers load a container bound for Beira. Radio Bristol and the Evening Post covered the story.

tools and manual typewriters which were distributed to schools, health centres, community and women's groups.

This first container was followed by another in December 1999 which had educational material (much of it from Portway Community and Luckwell primary schools) including 22 computers with printers, and another container in May 2002 with more teaching materials, including 100 computers, 1,200 national census bags, sports equipment, sewing materials and tools for the technical college.

Sending containers was never intended to be the main focus of the newly formed Link, however; instead, its aim was to help build a sustainable future as a way of tackling Beira's extreme poverty. And it would do this through community-based projects that would empower the people of Beira.

"Part of our ethos has been to use local people and local organisations," says Paul. "We see our role as being facilitators and initiators rather than deliverers. We're about empowering people to do things themselves."

THE RENAMO DILEMMA

There were two facts which Bristol's anti-apartheid campaigners did not take into account in the early days, admits Steve: "The fact that they spoke Portuguese, and we didn't. And that during the civil war, the side that we had no sympathy with at all was Renamo – and Beira turned out to be their stronghold. That was an issue in the early days."

BLB's concerns were understandable: Mozambique was still, in 1990, embroiled in a bitter war that killed over one million people in fighting and starvation. And South Africa-backed Renamo was responsible for much of that suffering; so much, in fact, that the United Nations accused it of "one of the most brutal holocausts against ordinary human beings since the Second World War".

So how did they resolve that issue? "Just straight talking, really," says Steve. "Our primary concern was solidarity, practical support, people to people support and we made that plain pretty quickly. We found friends and allies in Beira, and some were not political figures but community organisations, and so on.

"We've also worked with a number of leading political figures, including the current mayor, who is now independent but was Renamo in the past and has awful memories of the civil war in relation to how his family suffered. In the last 10 years or so, the politics has not been an issue at all."

It was lucky, perhaps, that Bristol's campaigners did not realise Beira was dominated by the party they disliked so intensely. "If we had done thorough research and planning we might have chosen somewhere else," says Steve.

"With hindsight, our involvement has been a helpful contribution to the maturing of politics in Beira, without laying too big a claim on it. But the fact that we've stayed with it 20 years, and we've got a good network with a number of voluntary and community-based organisations and have maintained contact with a series of politicians, has been helpful as their politics have evolved."

BUILDING CLOSER CIVIC LINKS

BLB's contribution to "the maturing of politics in Beira" began early. In 1992 – the year the civil war finally ended – the newly formed Link brought Beira City Council President Lucas Renco to Bristol.

SUCCESSES AND FAILURES

After more than two decades' work, what has been the impact of BLB? Three people who were there at the start look back at what's been achieved.

STEVE STRONG: "Where we've been most successful is in establishing a good trusting relationship with people in Beira, who know we are in it for the long haul and that we are genuinely listening to their priorities and respectfully respond where we can.

"We've brought an understanding of life in a very different country to the people of Bristol and there are many, many young people in Bristol who have had their horizons broadened over the years.

"The disability work is fantastically useful and has real potential for supporting disabled people and generating employment. We've been able to offer practical support to people in Beira to help their emergence as a more prosperous and confident city.

"The biggest disappointment is that if we'd had more time and resources this end, we would have been able to do an awful lot more. That's been frustrating."

PAUL DUNN: "We've been to able to show solidarity

to the people of Beira and offer some practical help to people on the ground. As well as helping people achieve a better quality of life, we've kept the flag flying for internationalism – we are all one people.

"Personally, I've found immense joy and satisfaction at being able to do a little bit to help people rebuild their lives. I was brought up as an internationalist so, for me, having the opportunity to develop relationships with people in other parts of the world has been wonderful.

"The biggest difficulty is fundraising; it's increasingly hard for a small charity like BLB to operate in this area."

BEVIS MILLER: "The main aim was to give solidarity to Mozambique and we gave that in a moral sense, without question. And that was really important.

"We gave some material aid and we certainly educated people in the UK about the realities of apartheid and about what South Africa was doing in countries like Mozambique.

"Yes, there was a limit as to what material aid we could provide. But if the fact that you can only do a little bit is used as an excuse to do nothing, nobody would ever do anything in the world."

The former teacher and welder spent time with Bristol City Council officers where he was able to observe, among other things, "the way that budgets are drawn up following consultation with a number of bodies and people", according to a report.

Senor Renco also visited schools, health centres, businesses, the police service, the fire service, trade unions and Penal Reform International. A keen footballer as a boy, he greatly enjoyed watching Bristol City defeat Leicester City, and attended a barn dance which, he said, "offered me unforgettable moments of delight".

It was, all agreed, a very successful visit and fulfilled one goal considered important by the British Government – to strengthen the new Mozambican administration, which was then moving from a one-party to a multi-party system, by sharing the British approach to democracy and citizenship.

Six years later Beira asked Bristol for practical help in preparing for its first democratic municipal elections. In June 1998, Bristol's International Twinnings Association coordinator Alix Hughes accompanied two councillors and an officer from Bristol City Council to run a series of workshops in Beira for politicians, would-be councillors and officials – a potentially tricky exercise given the party in-fighting in Beira at the time, just six years after the end of a very bitter war.

In all, 27 people attended the workshops including representatives from the three main parties, Frelimo, Renamo and Unito Democratica. Feedback from the participants was very positive and the Bristol delegation felt it was "highly significant that, after so many years of violent conflict, the political parties came together in one room to talk about democracy and open government".

The delegation added: "The tensions apparent during the first morning were soon replaced by an atmosphere of co-operation and it is a tribute to the participants that they were able to put old enmities aside. It is also a reflection of their intense desire for peace and reconstruction."

In 2004 Felicio Pedro Zacarias, Governor of Sofala Province (of which Beira is the capital), and four Mozambican officials visited Bristol as part of a Foreign and Commonwealth Office trip looking at UK models of devolved government. The trip was considered to play a "significant role in encouraging Mozambique to continue to promote the rule of law [and] good governance".

In 2005 Beira executive mayor Daviz Simango visited Bristol and the following year the first official Bristol City Council delegation went out to Beira. Steve Strong, who went with them, was delighted to see clear signs of progress: "It was great to see major improvement in refuse collection, mosquito eradication teams in action, water pumps opening up in the poorer areas and HIV/AIDS educational slogans in prominent places."

In 2009 Jonito Jone, a representative of Beira's Technical Secretariat for the Administration of Elections, visited Bristol during the recent City Council and European Parliament elections to learn about the British process ahead of the Mozambican elections for the Presidency, National Government and Provincial Government in October 2009.

These civic and political links may not be the kind of sexy projects that attract headlines. But there's no doubt these contacts made

Jonito Jone presents Lord Mayor Councillor Christopher Davies with a carving from Beira.

an important contribution at a time when Mozambique was evolving politically.

ESTABLISHING SCHOOL PARTNERSHIPS

A great deal of effort in the early years went into establishing partnerships between schools in Bristol and Beira. These school links would become a major focus of BLB's work over the next two decades and one of the best ways of developing a sense of mutual respect and understanding among the ordinary people of Bristol and Beira.

As well as setting up school links, BLB began a range of educational projects, from developing teaching packs to creating programmes for teacher exchange visits and funding school refurbishment.

Bristol teachers meet with AJOMAC , the community based youth group which uses traditional culture to promote issues such as HIV awareness.

In 1995/96, for example, £2,000 was sent to help rebuild Beira's dilapidated Julius Nyerere Primary School; four years later, another £6,000 was provided to enable the Beira link schools to build desks and chairs and rebuild toilet blocks damaged in the 2000 floods, and similar amounts followed in subsequent years.

Establishing a relationship with schools nearly 6,000 miles away, where the language is Portuguese rather than English, was not easy. As the 1997 annual report recorded ruefully: "We have continued to maintain links with Beira and have made efforts to improve these. This has not been an easy process which distance, language and other factors have not helped."

That's why exchange visits came to be play such a vital way in cementing the relationship between schools. The first took place in June 1998, when three Bristol head teachers and a local education authority representative went to Beira.

That visit resulted in the first school links being established between Bristol and Beira schools:

Portway Community School in Shirehampton and Samora Machel school in Beira; St Thomas Moore in Horfield and Manga school in Beira; and Luckwell Primary in Bedminster and Matacuani in Beira.

In October that year Beira's Director of Education Luis Januario paid a reciprocal visit to Bristol, visiting schools and education officials over a two-week period, and unveiling the plaque that still can be found on College Green commemorating the Friendship link.

These two visits marked the start of a series of exchanges between Bristol and Beira teachers and education officials, which played an important role in forging partnerships.

In total almost 20 Bristol teachers have visited Beira – using British Council funding or paying for their own trips – and a dozen Beira teachers have visited Bristol, with benefits to professional and curriculum development in both cities.

Beira Director of Education Luis Januario with Lord Mayor Graham Robertson and Bristol pupils.

BLB CELEBRATES 10 YEARS – AND BEIRA IS HIT BY TRAGEDY

A decade after the Link started, BLB was preparing to celebrate its 10th anniversary with a host of activities in Bristol but the year turned out to be memorable for quite another reason. In early 2000 Mozambique was hit by massive floods that caused hundreds of deaths and made millions homeless.

While the most disastrous flooding was further south, Beira was battered by huge waves and high winds. Buildings, roads and bridges were swept away, crops destroyed, agricultural land contaminated by seawater and 20,000 cattle lost.

More than 600 schools were closed and 42 health units destroyed, including Beira Central Hospital, the second largest in the country. The World Bank estimated the cost of repairing the damage to Mozambique's infrastructure and industry at US$1billion.

By coincidence, four Beira heads and two teachers had arrived in Bristol on an exchange visit at precisely this time and immediately became the local focus of attention for the tragedy unfolding in Mozambique.

They gave moving press interviews, such as the one in the *Bristol Evening Post* headlined: "My country is drowning". Bristol's newest radio station, The Eagle, interviewed teacher Senor Jonito who gave a very graphic account of what was happening, and expressed an emotional thank you to Bristol for supporting Mozambique.

The Lord Mayor of Bristol Councillor Graham Robertson appealed for Bristol to give generously in view of the city's special friendship with Beira, to "help our brothers and sisters who are so far away but so much in our thoughts".

The appeal prompted an outpouring of benefit gigs and donations for Bristol's sister city. Chief among these was a huge donation from top Bristol band Massive Attack, which handed over a cheque for £22,000 to BLB. Massive Attack's Daddy G (Grant Marshall) and 3D (Robert Del

Naja) donated the licence money from their single *Angel*, used in a TV ad by Emporio Armani.

Bristol International Twinnings Association coordinator Alix Hughes recalls getting a telephone call at 6pm: could he go on the radio at 10pm that night to talk about the floods? "I was knackered and thought 'no'," he recalls. "But then I thought, 'if it could raise funds for help, I simply had to do it'.

"The DJ Paul Fordham had picked a load of Mozambican music and they'd done this fake news item where Bristol place names were juxtaposed with Mozambican names. It was really moving. The whole studio went silent and they started getting phone calls; it had generated all this emotion. So they said: 'We'll put on a concert', and it was a really good gig. The guys from Massive Attack were there and they got drunk and said: 'We'll match whatever you raise'! And that's how it happened."

In an interview at the time, Daddy G spoke of how "very moved" they'd been to see the flood images of Mozambique on TV earlier that year: "We wanted to help the Beira Fund and [licensing the single] is the quickest and most direct way for Massive Attack to do so. We were glad to help."

Daddy G and 3D of Massive Attack present a cheque for £22,000 to BLB at the Beira mural at Inkworks.

Massive Attack's money went mostly on improving school toilets, recalls Steve. "True to our form we didn't think about eye-catching, high profile projects. We asked local people what they wanted and most of it went on improving school toilets. I saw the before and after, and I can vouch for the fact that it was money well spent!"

Massive Attack was not alone in being moved by the images of flood-ravaged Mozambique in 2000. Hundreds of ordinary Bristolians stuck their hands in their pockets to raise money for the flood relief effort.

Benefit gigs were organised, including Easton Community Centre's 'From the Heart' event, which brought together poets from Poetry Can and Bristol's Black writers Group, and featured capoeira dance, bands, DJs and a raffle.

The Bristol Bierkeller hosted 'Bristol United for Mozambique', with a line-up of acts and celebrities to support Christian Aid's work in Mozambique. Bristol businesses also rallied round; Nick Park from Aardman Animation gave his full support, along with actor Tony Robinson, local branches of Tesco and Pizza Hut, and Bristol's two football teams, City and Rovers.

As one observer said at the time, the people of Bristol were asked for an unprecedented show of support and unity for Mozambique – and they did not disappoint.

BENEFITS OF TWINNING

While Bristolians rallied round to help their twin city, the benefits of twinning were affirmed in an article in local government publication *Linking News* in September 2000. It found twinning activities contributed more than £100,000 to the local economy through visitors, grants and volunteer time.

Bristolians might have mentioned another less tangible, but no less powerful, benefit: the sense of shared community and global citizenship that comes from a greater understanding of another culture and country. A report looking at the Bristol/

Inkworks in St Pauls was the venue for the first mural unveiled in Bristol celebrating the link.

Beira link, written for the Local Government International Bureau emphasised this aspect of the Friendship Agreement.It found that Bristol had "benefited greatly from its link with Beira", adding: "In Bristol, the link with Beira developed technical skills and knowledge, shared good practice, strengthened management and interpersonal skills, fostered cultural links, and increased awareness of cultural diversity and global citizenship issues as a result of various projects.

"Benefits to schools, as a whole, include using the link in lessons and projects to raise awareness about cultural diversity, fair trade, human rights and arts projects. Head teachers learned about leadership in challenging circumstances when they visited Beira, enabling them to examine their own leadership skills.

"Furthermore, teachers learned about issues relevant to the subjects they teach."

Of course, not everything was rosy. The report acknowledged the problem of communication difficulties: "Lack of communication infrastructure between Bristol and Beira, especially among students, is difficult and frustrating."

Such problems made the coordinator's role all the more important, it said: "The principle lesson learned from Bristol City Council's experience with the Link has been the importance for the council of appointing an officer responsible for international link activities. This provides better coordination between different departments and means Bristol City Council can be more proactive in its approach."

CULTURAL EXCHANGE

Alongside the school links, a key aspect of BLB's work since it was founded has been raising

BRISTOL TWINNING

Bristol is twinned with seven cities around the world. They are:

- Beira, Mozambique
- Bordeaux, France
- Guangzhou, China
- Hannover, Germany
- Oporto, Portugal
- Puerto Morazan, Nicaragua
- Tbilisi, Georgia

ORIGINS OF TWINNING

Town twinning has a long and honourable history. Incredibly, it actually dates back to 836, when the German city of Paderborn and the French city of Le Mans struck a friendship with each other, according to research by Inverness Town Twinning Committee.

However, it really took off after the Second World War as a way of building strong links and friendships with communities in other countries. For example, Coventry twinned with Stalingrad and Dresden as an act of peace and reconciliation, all three cities having been badly bombed during the war.

Bristol was one of the first UK cities to embrace twinning when five leading Bristol citizens made a goodwill visit to Hannover in Germany in 1947. The people of Bristol had heard that many children were unable to go to school in the bitter winter of 1947, because they had no shoes; they collected shoes and the Goodwill Mission took them to Hannover.

The Bristol-Hannover link continues today. It is, says the Bristol Hannover Council which runs it, a matter of pride in both cities that the link was the first of its kind and that it came spontaneously from the wishes of its own citizens.

AIMS OF TWINNING

Town twinning is aimed at fostering friendship and co-operation between cities. As well as enabling local governments to work more closely together to promote commercial ties, a very important aspect of twinning is to help people from different cultures and backgrounds understand each other.

BRISTOL/BEIRA LINK

Strictly speaking, the link with Beira, which started in 1990, is a friendship agreement rather than a formal twinning arrangement. The aim of the Bristol Link with Beira (BLB) is to bring mutual benefits to the peoples of both cities.

However, with extreme poverty in Beira, BLB also aims to build a sustainable future for the people of Beira through community-based projects that will help the people of Beira to become self-sufficient and empowered. Its main focus of activities are: education, health, gender, young people, disability, and culture.

BLB is managed through the Southern Africa Resource Centre (SARC), a Bristol-based registered charity. BLB also has two part-time development workers, one in Beira and one in Bristol.

SARC HAS TWO KEY AIMS:

- To improve understanding in the South West of England of Southern African art, culture, history and current affairs;
- To help people in Southern Africa suffering need, hardship or distress.

BRISTOL ACTSA

BLB also has close links to Bristol ACTSA (Action for Southern Africa) which was established in 1995 as the successor to the Bristol Anti-Apartheid Movement. The Anti-Apartheid Movement had been dissolved after the first democratic elections in South Africa in 1994, having achieved its aims.

However, many people wanted to continue campaigning to overcome the legacies legacies of apartheid in South Africa and in other countries in Southern Africa. Bristol ACTSA campaigns for peace, justice and solidarity.

awareness of Mozambican culture. To this end, it has brought musicians, dancers, storytellers, films and exhibitions to Bristol.

These events have become one of the strongest features of the Link. Steve Strong explains: "We wanted to make it as reciprocal as possible, we didn't want to make it all about the generosity of Bristol, which is one reason for bringing music over."

In October 2003, for example, young Beira musicians, including drummers from the group Djaaka, visited several Bristol schools, singing songs with the theme of slavery and leading drum and dance sessions with pupils.

Coordinator Shona Symons described the children's response as "quite phenomenal". She added: "The children don't have much contact with different cultures. It was fascinating and really interesting for them. The guys spoke little English but had a translator with them. They had gone out and killed the animals themselves to make skins for the drums!"

As well as enabling Beira musicians to play in Bristol, BLB has also brought Mozambican writers such as Lilia Momple and Mia Couto, and organised story-telling sessions – one of which involved the Mozambiquan High Commissioner Antonio Gumende – and craft activities at the Commonwealth and Empire Museum and Bristol Central Library.

Among BLB's most popular activities are the visits by Mozambican musician and storyteller Celso Paco who has become a regular fixture in Bristol schools' calendar since 2004, spending a couple of weeks a year here to run workshops and lead assemblies, tell stories and teach children Mozambican songs and musical instruments.

In 2005 BLB worked closely with Bristol City Council's museums services to ensure a British Museum exhibition, Throne of Weapons, made from decommissioned firearms by Mozambican artist Kester, came to Bristol. Alongside the exhibition at Bristol Museum, BLB helped organise a month-long series of educational and cultural activities focussed on the throne.

BLB has also organised film screenings. In 2007, for example, it brought the Mozambican film director, Gabriel Mondlane, chair of the Mozambican Association of Film-makers, to Bristol to show a series of his films as part of Bristol's Afrika Eye festival. Gabriel Mondlane's visit coincided with the 100th anniversary of the founding of Beira.

RECENT YEARS

In 2006 BLB appointed its first development worker in Beira, Catharine Bass, on a part-time basis. One of her tasks was to administer BLB's small grants of up to $200 per year per project. Money went to projects working with children and youth, people with disabilities, those living with HIV/AIDS, and a women's sewing project.

Examples of BLB's small grants include $1,500 to improve facilities at the School for the Deaf and $1,500 for a women's group to spend on wheelchairs and sewing machines. One year the Institute for the Blind received $500 for materials and $200 was provided to buy soap and disinfectants for prisoners in Beira prison.

Such small grants are an example of how effective at a grassroots level a small charity such as BLB can be. As Steve Strong says: "Our small grants work has a direct impact on people's lives in Beira."

THE FIRST BLB VOLUNTEERS

BLB's work was further bolstered when the first BLB volunteer from Bristol University went out to Beira in 2006. Kevin Seely, a Portuguese language student, spent four months there – an experience he recalls with great affection.

"I owe a lot to BLB," he says in an email from Nigeria where he is working for an NGO. "As a 20-year-old studying Portuguese in Bristol, I knew that I wanted to work in international development.

"BLB offered me the chance to get some

valuable experience that has helped me greatly in my career. I learned a lot about development during the four months that I helped to manage BLB's grants for social and economic development projects in Beira.

"Working in the slums was hard at times. You'd witness violence, hunger, sick children with very little prospect of seeing their fifth birthdays. You'd know that you couldn't help everyone. Being in one of Bristol's partner schools, in contrast, was always calming. The children were always excited to meet someone who had come from afar."

Since then, several language students from Bristol University's Department of Hispanic, Portuguese and Latin American Studies have followed in Kevin's footsteps, the latest being Joe Budge who went out in March 2012.

Changes have occurred in Bristol too in the last few years. In 2010, BLB employed development worker Forward Maisokwadzo, who was well known in Bristol as Chair of Bristol Zimbabwe Association and for his work with Refugee Action. One of his first activities was to help develop a website which promotes BLB's work with Beira – www.bristolbeiralink.org.

New members have been appointed to the board of trustees and in 2011, after 21 years' work with BLB, Paul Dunn retired as chair. His successor is Kenya-born Peninah Achieng, who was chair of St Paul's Carnival for four years and works in the health service in financial services.

FUTURE CHALLENGES

So what is the future for BLB? Paul Dunn says: "I hope BLB will continue to find ways to support people in Beira. It will always be small but I hope it will continue to work with local people and local organisations, and continue to demonstrate solidarity with the people of Beira."

One difficulty is it is increasingly hard for small players like BLB to get involved in this kind of work, he says: "We haven't been able to access the major funding streams and walking around

shaking tins to fundraise in Bristol is difficult."

Despite the challenges, Steve Strong believes there will always be opportunities for a charity like BLB: "The fact that we are quite versatile and flexible means there will always be room for us to manoeuvre."

BLB trustee Jose Sluijs-Doyle, who has 15 years' experience in international development in Southern Africa, including Mozambique, says small organisations can be "very effective" because they don't have all the rules and admin of a bigger organisation. "But you have to have a strong linking person on the ground; you have to get local people involved."

Increasing capacity on the ground is one of BLB's biggest challenges for the future, she adds: "Otherwise the risk is you keep struggling at a basic level."

Peninah Achieng agrees that improving capacity in Beira is a key issue for BLB in the months ahead – and is vital to ensuring long-term sustainability. Ultimately, it is about empowering people to develop themselves, she says.

To that end, BLB intends to set up a board of volunteers in Beira, similar to the one in Bristol, to "gather and drive some of the projects on the ground", she says. "This would be a legacy to ensure that we have a body that can continue."

Peninah and the board are passionate about BLB's work. "Personally speaking, Mozambique is very close to my heart because it's in Africa and I'm from Kenya," she says. "Also, if you look at its history, Mozambique has really suffered. We are a grassroots organisation and we see the impact of what we're doing on the ground, and that's very powerful."

THE BIGGER PICTURE

The friendship agreement with Beira arose out of the work of Bristol's anti-apartheid campaigners. Bevis Miller, then chair of the Bristol Anti-Apartheid Committee, describes the bigger political picture that lay behind the link.

Back in the 1980s South Africa was running a campaign against what were termed the frontline states – Mozambique, Zambia, Tanzania and Angola. It was putting enormous pressure on those countries, economically, politically and with military interventions, to ensure they didn't provide the liberation movements of southern Africa, particularly the ANC, with any safe havens.

The pressure got very acute. There were letter bombs, car bombs, commandos being dropped over the borders to carry out assassinations. The United Nations' Special Committee on Apartheid called on the international community to oppose apartheid and also to provide solidarity with those countries. In Bristol we decided to try to get a formal agreement between Bristol City Council and a Mozambican city, and we chose Beira because it is a port, like Bristol, and there'd been some history of trading between us.

Bristol City Council was very supportive; it was really important to us that this didn't become a party political issue. The council was Labour-run but I must pay tribute to Sir Robert Wall, then leader of the Conservatives, who gave it his full support, and in fact when it went to council it had the support of all three parties.

The council set up a committee to deal with international relations and that became very important. There was a campaign for local authorities to declare themselves apartheid-free zones and the motion was put to Bristol City Council but no one had thought through the implications. The council owned Bristol City Docks at Avonmouth and the dockers were obviously worried about their jobs. I took representatives of the South African trades union movement to a public meeting of the dockers, which was interesting; they certainly spoke their minds!

They were appalled, most of them, at the horrors of apartheid and wanted to do something but didn't feel they should lose their jobs to salve other people's consciences.

So the council funded a piece of research to look at Bristol's trade patterns with South Africa. We found it was mainly South African coal coming through the docks and the importer agreed to switch to Chinese coal. So within two or three years we had dramatically changed the trading patterns and that was very positive.

We can delude ourselves with the over-importance of what we did; the South African people liberated themselves, fundamentally. But having said that, the work of the international community in solidarity with the liberation struggles was, the ANC would say, crucial in terms of giving moral and practical support.

It was incredibly important to Beira, which was under desperate pressure, to know there were people in a city like Bristol that supported them. The fact, for example, that the Mozambican Ambassador came and spoke to Bristol City Council was really important to people in Mozambique.

Bevis Miller with the Lord Mayor of Bristol Cllr Jim Williams and Ambassador Panguene.

THE VIEW FROM BEIRA

Catharine Bass is BLB's representative in Beira. She has spent over a decade in Beira, where she also works for VSO. She assesses the key challenges facing the city.

Q: What are the three biggest challenges facing the people of Beira?
The three biggest problems are…

POVERTY – While there appears to be more money around, a large proportion of people in Beira still live in extreme poverty, find it impossible to get employment and do not have the capacity to start their own small businesses (either through lack of confidence, skills or start up funds). Prices for basic foodstuffs have increased considerably in recent years, and more families struggle to have a decent diet.

EDUCATION – While primary education is free to all, there aren't enough secondary school and university places, and the cost is prohibitive for some people. The quality of education is also a concern due to a lack of well-trained teachers, lack of educational resources and large class sizes.

HEALTH – in particular HIV/AIDS, which will continue to have a big impact in Beira. While it is great that more awareness and access to anti-retroviral drugs is leading to people living longer, this will create more demands on an already stretched health service.

Q: What kind of difference can a small charity such as BLB make in a place like Beira?
A small charity is generally able to be more flexible and more personal. It can look at individual cases and support small Mozambican organisations that may not be considered by the large NGOs, thereby working much closer to local people, responding to their needs and desires rather than concentrating on policies and national campaigns. This more hands-on approach can

be more interesting for supporters as they can see the direct impact of their work on real people.

Q: What in your view has been BLB's most effective activity?
Probably the wheelchair initiative in which two men were trained in Tanzania for a year to make high quality wheelchairs from local materials. While the programme is still in a development stage and there are many challenges, people now have access to appropriate wheelchairs and there is much greater awareness concerning the issue.

This initiative prompted and financed through the link has meant that Beira has the only qualified technician and only centre in the whole of Mozambique producing appropriate chairs. Though through our awareness raising, we hope more people will be trained in other cities as the demand is so great.

Q: What can we in Bristol learn from the people of Beira?
We could learn to…

VALUE EDUCATION MORE. As a result of many years when it was impossible to access education, people who missed out are now trying to catch up. At all levels, from primary up to university, adults are enrolled and studying hard. A large proportion of people who work are also studying, giving up their free time to try and get to the next level. There is still great respect for teachers and the annual national Teachers Day is celebrated throughout the country.

DEAL WITH GRIEF AND DEATH AS PART OF LIFE. I think the way Mozambicans grieve and then get on with life is something we could learn from. Death, illness and suffering is so common here that Mozambique would cease to function if people did not have a way of dealing with this issue. Grief is very real and sometimes extreme but tends to be concentrated in a shorter period of

time and is much more openly displayed and shared. Anniversaries are remembered with services and family get-togethers but daily life continues, people are talked about with their names preceded by 'the departed … ', and death is not seen as something unusual or strange.

HAVE AMBITIONS AND FIGHT TO ACHIEVE THEM. Whether through education or starting small (sometimes minute) businesses, many Mozambicans are trying to improve their lives. This can be seen by the number of people building houses; for many, this will be a very slow process, literally a few blocks at a time, but the thought of having the security of their own home drives them on.

HAVE FUN AND BE CHEERFUL. Mozambicans have fun sometimes in the face of overwhelming adversity. Given the problems faced by Mozambicans – the poverty, the loss of loved ones, the struggle to access basic human rights – they could be forgiven for being miserable and complaining. But while they can complain as much as anyone, there is a level of cheerfulness, friendliness, humour and optimism that is different from my experience of the UK.

CAMPAIGNING ACTIVITIES IN BRISTOL

"On a dead tree there are no monkeys'"
– Mozambican proverb

Bristol Link with Beira was born out of a campaigning organisation – the Bristol Anti-Apartheid Committee – so it's hardly surprising to find that BLB is just as vocal on the issues it cares passionately about.

Issues such as poverty and debt, for example. BLB was an enthusiastic supporter of the Jubilee Debt Campaign, and its predecessor Jubilee 2000, which were set up to demand an end to the scandal of poor countries paying money to the rich world, leaving millions of people enslaved by debts their countries could never repay.

In 2005, BLB took part in Oxfam's Make Poverty History campaign, which saw Deputy Lord Mayor of Bristol, Royston Griffey, and Cardinal Uwishaka, Oxfam's Mozambique Country Director, firing arrows at a giant archery target in front of Bristol City Council for a photo call. The target represented the Millennium Development Goals – the pledge made in 2000 by 189 nations to free people from extreme poverty and multiple deprivations. BLB was also very active in awareness-raising on issues such as trade injustice. In 2004 it brought sugar farmers to Bristol – which was declared a Fairtrade City a year later – to talk to school children and the wider public about the problems they were experiencing.

Two years ago, in 2010, BLB brought Fairtrade cashew and peanut producer Isobel Antonio to deliver workshops and assemblies to Bristol schools during Fairtrade Fortnight. She spoke to more than 3,000 pupils and was able to tell them how much difference being a Fairtrade supplier had made to her and her community.

Isabel had barely travelled outside her village before, let alone UK, but was a great ambassador for her country and the ideals of the fair trade movement. She told her audiences that as a direct result of producing food for Fairtrade, her community now received three times the amount of income from their nut trees,. Their children were no longer malnourished; families could afford to buy bicycles to make it easier for children (who often have to walk a long way) to get to school.

Cardinal Uwishaka, Oxfam's Mozambique country director, missing the World Development Targets with Dep Mayor Cllr Royston Griffey.

Isabel Antonio, Fairtrade Producer, with Lord Mayor Cllr Christopher Davies.

FUNDRAISING ACTIVITIES

BLB has been grateful to have the support of a dedicated band of individuals who have worked hard to raise funds for its work. Over the years, many people have taken part in a sponsored walk or run, attended a talk, joined other supporters for a meal, or simply donated money.

The Meals for Mozambique are BLB's main annual fund-raising activity, and are usually hosted by one of BLB's partner schools. As well as food, they often also include music or storytelling, or a talk such as the one attended by Dawn Primarolo MP, which focussed on how Bristol could offer long term support to help achieve sustainable development.

In 2007, for example, the organisation held two Meals for Mozambique at Colston Primary School which raised more than £1,600. The first meal featured the first showing in Britain of the film,

Marranbantando – the stories my guitar sings', described as "a sort of Mozambican *Buena Vista Social Club*", while the second meal included a performance and storytelling from Celso Paco.

Other fund-raising activities involve rather more effort... and sweat. In September 2011, a team of five half-marathon runners took part in Bristol Half Marathon, raising £1,696 towards setting up a regional wheelchair workshop in Beira in the process.

The team included three Zimbabweans. Explaining why they were involved, Forward Maisokwadzo, a Zimbabwean and BLB's Bristol development worker, said: "The port of Beira is really Zimbabwe's access to the sea and so there are strong economic and historical links between our country and the people of Beira. We all felt we wanted to get behind this mobility project in Beira as a way of supporting sustainable development there."

In 2008, BLB produced its first calendar, featuring lovely images from Beira. It was enthusiastically received and has become a regular feature of its fundraising strategy.

BOTTLE CUTTING PROJECT

Members of the environmental youth organisation Ajomac turn old bottles into crafts to be sold to earn a little revenue. With funding from Bristol ACTSA in 2008, BLB paid for training, a couple of bottle-cutting kits and essential equipment such as a table and safety gloves.

A peaceful future and a future without AIDS

HEALTH

"A man does not run among thorns for no reason; either he is chasing a snake or a snake is chasing him"
Mozambican proverb

HIV/AIDS IN BEIRA

Of all the serious diseases affecting Mozambique, HIV/AIDS is the greatest threat to the nation's development, according to UNICEF Mozambique.

Mozambique has the 10th highest prevalence rate in the world, at around 16% of the population. Sofala Province, where Beira is located, has even higher prevalence, with more than a quarter (26%) infected with HIV, according to UNICEF.

The main reason is the high level of migration along the Beira transport corridor from the port to Zimbabwe and beyond. Transport corridors are known to increase the prevalence of HIV/AIDS because of a constant influx of truck drivers and commercial sex workers.

Young women are particularly vulnerable to infection, says BLB trustee and HIV in Africa consultant Jose Sluijs-Doyle: "In 2005, 22% of women aged 20-24 were HIV positive compared to 7% of men. This demonstrates the disproportionate vulnerability to HIV for women.

"Also, there is the significant burden of care that mostly falls on women and young girls. This in turn limits their chances to get education and other opportunities in life."

American academic Kenly Greer Fenio, who spent a year in Mozambique in 2007 researching HIV/AIDS, describes Mozambique's HIV prevalence rates as "nothing short of a disaster".

"Many companies in the region are now forced to train two or three new employees for the same job, as it is virtually guaranteed that at least one will die," she says in her research paper, Between Bedrooms and Ballots: The Politics of HIV's 'Economy of Infection' in Mozambique.

HIV/AIDS FAST FACTS

MOZAMBIQUE
- Mozambique has the 10th highest HIV/AIDS prevalence rate in the world
- There are around 1.6 million people living with HIV and AIDS – compared to 85,000 in the UK
- The prevalence rate for adults aged 15 to 49 is around 16.2% – compared to 0.2% in the UK
- The province with the highest infection rate is Sofala (Beira is situated in Sofala Province), at around 26.5%
- Infection rates among women aged 20-24 are four times as high as men the same age
- UNICEF Mozambique estimates by now around 626,000 children have lost one or both parents to AIDS-related illnesses

(Figures: UNICEF Mozambique and UNAIDS)

"Parents and teachers, two of the most stabilising forces on the continent, are hardest hit. This does not bode well for the rapidly growing number of orphans or the extended families already bursting at the financial seams that cannot manage yet another child who has lost both parents."

AN ORPHAN CRISIS

UNICEF Mozambique has warned of an "orphan crisis of alarming dimensions". UNICEF believes the number of children who have lost one or both parents to HIV/AIDS will soon rise to more than 600,000.

In 2004 the government declared HIV/AIDS a national emergency, the epidemic having reduced life expectancy from 41 years in 1999 to 38.1 years in 2004. A major health campaign is underway, aided by an international effort in recent years to make anti-retroviral drugs cheaper in developing countries, and aims to make treatment available to all HIV/AIDS patients. But as of 2008 fewer than half of those who needed anti-retrovirals were getting them.

THE CURSE OF POVERTY

Poverty is a major burden in tackling HIV/AIDS because if people can't afford to eat properly, it is harder for them to recover from the opportunistic infections that affect people with HIV, says Jose.

"Treatment has helped a lot of people live a normal life for longer – if they have nutrition. Good nutrition means you can lead a healthy lifestyle and remain economically viable," she adds. "If

RAYS OF HOPE IN BEIRA

Kevin Seely spent six months in Beira in 2006 as the first Bristol University language student to volunteer for BLB. He recorded his observations in this report.

An eight-foot tall witchdoctor walks on to the stage. Amidst spellbinding dances and captivating rhythms, the man's voice beckons down accusingly on the audience. "Who of you here doesn't wear a condom?" The theatre is silent.

Not only in the Casa de Cultura do they talk, sing, dance and chant about AIDS, but in Mozambique's newspapers, workplaces, marketplaces and even in the streets. In Beira, twinned with Bristol since 1990, HIV/ AIDS is thought to have infected 20-40% of the population.

It was because of the twinning I got the chance to get closer to the realities of life in Beira. I worked mostly with community-based development projects, also on educational and cultural links between our cities.

From a massage project that gives blind women a chance to work their way out of poverty to a sewing cooperative set up in response to mass redundancies at a textile factory, each of the initiatives we support serves as a living example of determination and innovation to fight poverty.

A particularly inspirational story is that of Amai Mussananhi, recently strengthened thanks to £500 donated from the Walk for Southern Africa.

Amai is a group of women who organise before and after-school activities for around 40 orphans in one of the harshest slums in Beira. Many of the children lost parents to HIV/AIDS and find themselves dependent on older siblings or grandparents, selling fruit and nuts at the roadside to raise family income.

. With the Walk's funds, we rehabilitated Amai's crumbling activity centre, bought benches and a table and started sewing and drama lessons. As part of a wider psychological support, these orphan children are learning to talk, sing, draw and paint about the disease. With luck, they might one day find themselves in the Casa de Cultura.

If children don't have enough food and a balanced diet, it makes it hard to recover from infections.

you don't have good nutrition, or you become weakened because you are ill and you can't work your land or you lose your job, you end up in a vicious cycle of poverty."

BLB'S WORK ON HIV

In 2010 Bristol Link with Beira worked with Coaching For Hope to bring HIV awareness and life skills training to young people through their passion for football. BLB has also funded work with AIDS orphans in the Munghava district of Beira over several years. Children are taught literacy skills and basic English as well as also basket making and sewing using a machine. They use these skills to earn money and are often seen selling baskets and handkerchiefs after school.

BLB also supported Rudho ni Upenhi, an association of people living with AIDS which started in 2002 and has more than 100 members, with funds for a sewing project and furniture to help them with their meetings and trainings.

OTHER HEALTH PROBLEMS

Apart from HIV/AIDS, the main health threats are malaria, sleeping sickness, malnutrition caused by poverty and diarrhoea caused by water-borne diseases.

More children die of malaria than any other disease in Mozambique, according to UNICEF Mozambique.

It accounts for 60 per cent of paediatric hospital admissions and 30 per cent of hospital deaths, and it is a major reason why Mozambique still has one of the world's highest child mortality rates. Here, too, poverty plays a key role, says Jose, because most people can't afford to buy mosquito nets.

ACCESS TO HEALTH CARE

After independence in 1975, the government created a free, nationalised health care system and established a series of clinics to provide basic health services. However, around 800 of these clinics were destroyed in the war.

In the last 20 years, the government has invested a great deal of money re-establishing the network of clinics but access to health services is still limited. Only 40% of the population has access to health facilities and only about one person in three lives within 30 miles of the nearest health unit. Medical staff are very overstretched, with around three doctors per 100,000 people compared to 274 per 100,000 in the UK.

People have to walk for hours to access treatment, not just for HIV/AIDS but for other services such as maternity, says Jose: "People are literally walking for two days while in labour. That's not unique to Mozambique; it's true of a lot of African rural areas."

COACHING FOR HOPE: USING FOOTBALL TO PREVENT HIV/AIDS

In October 2010 a group of very excited boys and girls gathered in Beira to play football – a passion very close to their hearts. Leading the session were two professional football coaches from Bristol.

Bristol City Football Club had released Damian Hodge and Dave McGibbon on full pay to train 30 volunteer coaches in Beira as part of an extraordinary programme called Coaching for Hope which uses football to get messages about HIV/AIDS to young people.

It is run by Skillshare International, a UK NGO with an excellent track record in Southern Africa, which was invited into the project by BLB. The six-day coaching programme also included Provida, a Mozambique-based life skills organisation that uses street football to reach out to the poorest parts of Beira.

HIV and AIDS are the major health issue in Beira and Sofala Province. Beira has one of the highest HIV prevalence rates in Southern Africa and young people are particularly vulnerable.

Coaching for Hope brings professional coaches from the UK to train local coaches to recognised FA standards. At the same time, they are taught to use football drills to empower young people to protect themselves from HIV, unwanted pregnancy, and sexually transmitted infections.

The strategy works brilliantly well, says Dave McGibbon. "Football is an incredibly powerful medium because everyone plays it," he says. "It was really easy to get the messages over – the children completely understood them."

The project was sponsored by Bristol 2018 (Bristol's bid to host World Cup football in 2018), BLB and consultancy firm Tribal. A container of donated football shirts was also sent out from Bristol and handed out to participants.

Dave and Damian trained 30 local volunteer coaches; the plan was for them to train 500-600 girls and boys aged 10-20. Although they soon discovered the local coaches had "an absolute minimum of equipment and resources", the Bristol City coaches were very struck by their attitude and commitment, says Damian.

"Their enthusiasm and desire to learn was inspiring and they responded exceptionally well to the programme which was a real success," he says. "The trip was truly memorable experience and highly rewarding both professionally and personally."

The young people were desperate to attend the course, says Dave. He recalls how one girl was

Youngsters and volunteer coaches taking part in the Coaching for Hope programme.

so keen that she used the bus money she'd been given by the project organisers to buy a pair of football boots. "She was walking nine kilometres a day in bare feet to take part in the course and nine kilometres back home again!" he recalls.

One of the key messages was the longevity of the disease, says Dave: "We had a football game in which three people were shooters and the rest defenders. No matter how long it took, sooner or later a ball would get past them.

"We had one team who defended really well but in the end they got tired. We told them, that's what happens to your body; it tires of the disease. Whether it's three years, or five years, or 10 years, it will get you."

The 10 days the Bristol City coaches spent in Beira had a big impact. Both were shocked by the poverty but also struck by "the way the Mozambicans were about adversity – they were all so positive about things", says Dave. As for Damian, it was the resourcefulness of the Mozambican people – "just simply making the most out of what they have" – that impressed him.

Dave and Damian returned to Bristol convinced of the value of what they'd been doing. Damian says: "The importance of the HIV/AIDS awareness programme was evident to us everyday and we felt privileged to be involved in the project."

Beira has left its mark on Dave. He recalls the moment the coach of a Beira football team arrived at the stadium they were using. "He arrived on a bicycle with 20 footballs – all pumped up – and all the cones and bibs, his water, all of this on his bicycle!" he says.

"I never complain now about how much kit I've got to carry; I've not complained since I got back from Beira! It was a tremendous experience."

Damian Hodge and Dave McGibbon from Bristol City FC were released on full pay to coach 30 volunteer coaches in Beira.

HOPE FOR LANDMINE VICTIMS

Landmines were laid in Mozambique with vicious enthusiasm during the last century. By the time peace arrived in 1990, Mozambique had around three million landmines, according to the International Campaign to Ban Landmines. The tragedy of landmines is they remain dangerous after the fighting has ended, not only killing and injuring civilians but also making land unusable for decades. Children are particularly at risk of injury.

Mozambique's land mine legacy means it has a high number of disabled people who have lost limbs to mines. There's an urgent need for equipment such as prosthetic limbs, wheelchairs and crutches to help disabled people get around.

As the Backwell-based charity Motivation UK says: "In developing countries, people with mobility disabilities are commonly the most vulnerable and excluded members of society. Without an appropriate wheelchair, they can't leave their homes, go to school or get a job. And they are at risk of potentially fatal secondary health complications like pressure sores."

One of BLB's most inspiring projects has been to work with Motivation as well as AJODEMO, the local Association of Young Disabled, to set up a purpose-built workshop in Beira to provide wheelchairs for the central region of Mozambique.

BLB sent two Beira volunteers to Tanzania for a year to learn to design and produce custom-made chairs for landmine victims, polio sufferers and people with work injuries. One of the volunteers, Jorge, not only passed his exams with flying colours but has started making wheelchairs in Beira.

Motivation UK says second hand wheelchairs can seem like a logical solution to the lack of wheelchairs in poor countries. "But in reality, they are part of the problem – simply because they haven't been designed to be used in developing countries.

"Most quickly break, can't be easily repaired and, because they don't fit their user properly, can cause serious health problems. Some of these health problems – like pressure sores – can be life-threatening."

First wheelchair recipient Johane Joaquim Joao.

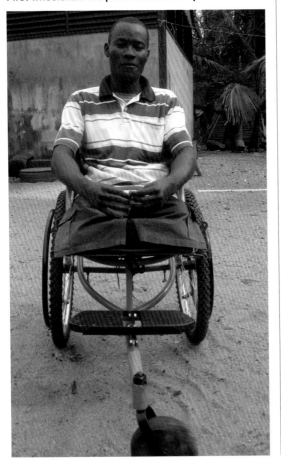

THE WHEELCHAIR MAKER

Jorge, 31, really enjoys the work, he told BLB volunteer Joe Budge: "It's very good, I really enjoy helping disabled people.

"It's important that the wheelchairs are made in Beira instead of being imported from abroad because we make sure the wheelchair fits them exactly and if there is a problem they can come back and we know the wheelchair and how to fix it."

Jorge's biggest problem is that not enough people know of his business, he says: "I'd really like to increase awareness of the business so that everyone knows about it."

THE WHEELCHAIR USER

Johane Joaquim Joao, 25, who had both legs amputated from above the knee as a child after an illness, was one of the first people to benefit from one of Jorge's wheelchairs.

He told Joe the wheelchair had made a real difference to him. "It's good. It is made of very strong material and is a better model than the other ones and also it is not so expensive.

The wheelchairs are made to fit the users.

"Before, I had one that was old and almost broken. It was heavy and someone had to push me. In this one I can go out by myself whenever I want, it gives me independence."

"There's a wealth of amputation waiting in the ground"

Singer Bruce Cockburn in his song *The Mines of Mozambique*

This line in Bruce Cockburn's song took Canadian doctor Colleen O'Connell to Mozambique in 2000 to study the effects of landmines on the population. She found the legacy of war meant Mozambicans continued "to risk life and limb as they venture out in search of water, firewood and access to their farmland".

In Canada, as in the UK, most amputations are the result of vascular or infectious causes; in Mozambique, 99% were caused by trauma. These were mostly landmines but also bullet wounds and machete injuries. Children were particularly vulnerable as they played in fields around their homes.

Yet, despite the years of trauma and tragedy, what struck Dr O'Connell was the optimism and energy of the people. In an article written for the Canadian Medical Association, she said: "Although the personal accounts and physical scars of the Mozambicans I interviewed and examined were horrific, I felt that I would be doing them an injustice by victimising them further, promoting the image of a bleak, grief-stricken Africa.

"Each individual story was unique: tales of community, heroism and survival against all odds. The woman who lost both legs when she was running to escape rebel fighters, and ran over mines that her family had set to protect her village, now manages her family and farm from her knees wearing bright orange plastic kneecap protectors.

"A soldier who had lost both legs in a landmine explosion is active in an organisation for disabled soldiers, runs a community store and farms. The girl whose arm was hacked off with a machete and handed back to her is now training to become a traditional medicine woman.

"These strong people could teach us lessons about the power of people to endure and forgive. The healing process of a country is a long, slow one, not the stuff of headlines, much like rehabilitation medicine itself. I feel privileged to have been able to witness this."

BUILDING LINKS BETWEEN PEOPLE WITH LEARNING DISABILITIES

BLB has always tried to focus on people on the margins of society. Few people are more discriminated against, wherever they are, than people with learning disabilities.

In Beira, where facilities are scarce, their plight is particularly difficult. Which was why, when in 2005 BLB came across a group of parents who wanted to build a day centre to care for their children, it was keen to help.

The organisation's name, ACRIDEME – the Association for Mentally Deficient Children – showed how different attitudes in Beira were towards people with learning disabilities.

But far more shocking is the fact that back then there weren't any people with learning disabilities above the age of 22. "As we understood it, many had been killed in the civil war – either murdered because of their disability or simply unable to survive in those circumstances," says Steve Day, communications director for Brandon Trust.

Brandon Trust got involved after BLB treasurer Steve Strong approached them for help. Brandon Trust works throughout the South West supporting approximately 1,200 people with learning disabilities to live the lives they choose. Taking part in an overseas project was a new venture for them but Brandon Trust decided to support ACRIDEME with a small grant over five years.

"It was comparatively small but it made a great deal of difference in Beira," he recalls. "Although Mozambique had been coming together as a democracy since the end of the civil war, there

BLB worked with a group of parents who wanted to build a day centre for children with learning disabilities.

was still very little being done for people with learning disabilities.

Visiting Beira had a profound effect on Steve personally. "I've travelled a great deal and I've also worked with people with learning disabilities practically all my life," he say. "But the poverty in Beira was harsh and the circumstances for people with learning disabilities very difficult indeed. It was glaringly obvious that people were often just left alone, without any resources or anything to do.

"We visited a hospital with many people with profound learning disabilities, which was very depressing. There were open wards and shared toileting, no personal space at all, very little in the way of individual clothing and no meaningful occupation. Lots of people were rocking and there was some self-harming. From my perspective it was very institutionalised, though I realise the staff were struggling with a terrible lack of resources.

"People with learning disabilities, whether in Mozambique or UK, are often at the bottom of the social care agenda. In this country, people with disabilities can sometimes voice their issues but for people with learning disabilities, being able to express their situation is much more difficult because of cognitive impairment and verbal communication difficulties."

Brandon Trust's project with ACRIDEME has ended now but it was a positive experience.

"We did a 24-hour drumming marathon to raise money, where people with learning disabilities and staff kept drumming right through the night. It was a great experience and many people with learning disabilities took part for whom Africa hadn't touched their radar," recalls Steve.

"It was a way of demonstrating that learning disabilities are not just a UK phenomenon but reach out across the world – and that people with learning disabilities can do something for other people; they are not just victims but can contribute meaningfully."

WOMEN

"He who led me in the night will be thanked by me at daybreak"
Mozambican proverb

AMAI MUSSANANHI

BLB's work with the woman's organisation Amai Mussananhi shows how far small amounts of money can go in making a real difference to people's lives. Amai Mussananhi – which means women helping women (literally one women holding up another) – was established in 1995 as a self-help organisation for women throughout Sofala province.

Its objectives are to promote women's rights and equality, especially in rural areas. These include promoting women's education and opportunities for women to develop skills that will help them become economically independent.

Amai Mussananhi also provides healthcare – especially in the areas of cholera, HIV/AIDS and child nutrition – and works to increase awareness of landmines which still contaminate large areas of the Mozambican countryside and cause such suffering, especially to children as they walk to school, play or help in the fields.

All training is done by local recruits and everyone is a volunteer; no one is paid for their work. In over two decades of working, Amai Mussananhi has become very experienced in gaining access to rural villages and making contact with women there.

In Beira, one of Amai Mussananhi's core activities is to support children orphaned as a result of HIV/AIDS. They do so by organising before and after school activities for around 40 orphans living in some of Beira's harshest slums.

These children are dependent on older siblings or grandparents, selling fruit and nuts on the roadside for income. (Read Kevin Seeley's pen

BLB works with women and children to help the youngsters get into school which can act as a step ladder out of poverty.

portraits of some of these children for a glimpse into their lives.)

Since 1999, BLB's sister organisation Bristol ACTSA (Action for Southern Africa) had regularly donated £500 a year to Amai, raised through its annual fundraising 'Walk for Southern Africa'. This was increased to £900 in 2006 and £1,000 in 2008. The 'Walk', originally called the 'Soweto Walk', started in 1980 and has taken place every year since, raising thousands of pounds for projects and campaigning in South and Southern Africa. It takes place in Priddy in June – for further information contact Sheila Roberts (0117 9719912).

As well as being used to help fund Amai Mussananhi's work with vulnerable children, these small grants also enabled them to buy a property, thus securing their future. They are able to sub-let the building at weekends which gives them a small amount of much-needed income.

Bristol ACTSA stepped in again in 2010 with a small £500 grant which went to support activities with younger children (so 30 of the children get a snack and two facilitators are paid), which they also used to help some widows in the local area to learn a new skill. Other funding has been used to support Amai's craft project which helps bring in extra revenue.

The money also enabled Amai Mussananhi to provide practical support to seven children who were entering High School for the first time by supplying them with uniforms, shoes, books, pens. The organisation was also able to ensure all its children began the day with a simple breakfast.

Pens, shoes, books, breakfast: they are such small benefits in one sense but they are huge in another. The support these children receive at Amai Mussananhi means a huge amount to youngsters living in some of the most difficult of circumstances, and enabling them to go to school may provide a step-ladder out of poverty and to a better future.

PRACTICAL HELP TO THOSE WHO MOST NEED IT

Earlier this year BLB volunteer Joe Budge visited Amai Mussanahi to see for himself how the link with BLB was working. He spoke to Oussiana, a member of Amai Mussananhi for several years.

JOE: "How has the link with BLB benefited Amai Massananhi?"

OUSSIANA: "Since the link began, there have been projects like the one last year which helped the people suffering from HIV/AIDS and they benefited through food supplied by Bristol. And also the children have benefited a lot from scholarships, by getting into schools (there are three in Samora Machel and three in Sao Temba) and through being supplied with school equipment."

JOE: "What difference has the link made to your members?"

OUSSIANA: "The big change is that people with HIV now have food to eat every day. Before the support they were not able to afford to have food every day."

JOE: "What have you liked/enjoyed most about the link with Bristol?"

OUSSIANA: "Difficult question. The best thing about Bristol is that they always help during difficult times and all the help Bristol does is incredibly important."

JOE: "What are your hopes for the future for the link?"

OUSSIANA: "Our hopes for the future are that they continue to help us so that we can keep on growing. Maybe we could do with some help for the pre-school children with buying snacks and teaching equipment."

AMAI MUSSANANHI: A VOLUNTEER'S PERSPECTIVE

ABLB volunteer Leila Bright visited Amai Mussananhi in 2008.

I worked as a volunteer in Beira for around five weeks in August 2008. My work was very rewarding in terms of learning both Portuguese and the way in which charity organisations are managed and run on the ground.

Because the organisation in Beira consists of only three workers who coordinate the distribution and administration of funds and exchange trips from Bristol, I had to find my own way of travelling around the city to the various groups which gave me a real sense of both the social and spatial geography of Beira.

Though the work was at times challenging, I felt that this is one of the few organisations I have come across where funds donated go directly into the projects they were intended for, rather than being used to cushion volunteers or support the overhead costs of the organisation itself.

In terms of the work I did, I spent time with a few groups around the city, concentrating mainly on a volunteer youth group, Ajomac, and the women and orphan project, Amai Mussananhi. Amai Mussananhi are a small collective who work with orphans providing a space within which the children can have lessons when teachers are available, learn practical skills such as sewing and basket weaving and just have fun – drawing, singing, dancing, etc.

The centre itself consists of a large room with a few chalkboards and very useful number of benches organised by Kevin Seely (a previous volunteer). Although the resources are sparse, I felt that the children, who live nearby, appreciated having something to do in the afternoon and there seemed to be a system whereby the older kids looked after the younger ones when teachers were not available.

I had the pleasurable job of giving art lessons to the kids twice a week and documenting the state of the group in order to make a report back to BLB when I returned. When I left, securing the ownership of the centre by Amai Mussananhi seemed to be in the works along with the sewing and selling clothes that the children had a hand in making under the guidance of a local tailor.

Leila Bright worked with orphans at the Amai Mussananhi project where the children can learn skills as well as enjoying singing and dancing.

PORTRAIT OF HOPE:
THE CHILDREN OF AMAI MUSSANANHI

I n 2007, BLB volunteer Kevin Seely compiled this brief profile of some of the vulnerable children being cared for by Amai Massananhi. All have lost one or both parents to HIV or AIDS and most live in some of the poorest bairros (neighbourhoods) in Beira – the slums of Goto and Espungara.

And while all are now going to school, quite a few have missed years of schooling. Kevin explains: "Unlike in Britain when most children start school at five and progress automatically from one year to the next, in Mozambique this progression depends on passing exams at the end of the year.

"More importantly, the school must have sufficient capacity to enrol the pupil in a higher class. As a result, students often 'miss' years, particularly those who are more vulnerable."

Angelina, seven, lives in the Goto bairro with her aunt, brother and grandfather. Their home is made of concrete blocks and bamboo. She's been going to Amai Mussananhi for two years. Both her parents died when she was young and she depends on her grandfather's state pension. She is in her second year of school where her favourite subjects are maths and Portuguese.

Ancha, 10, has been attending Amai Mussananhi for two years. He is in his fourth year at school and attends the centre in his free time, where he enjoys playing and weaving. He lives with his grandfather, aunt and uncle. His parents separated when he was young and he was living with his mother until she died. His father is still alive but lives separately with his sister.

Paulina was three when her father died. Her mother worked in the local hospital as a cook and Paulina dreams that she too will work there, maybe as a doctor. Her house is made of concrete and bamboo and has two bedrooms and a front room. She sleeps with her mother while her older brother and sister share the other room. Her aunt, uncle and grandfather sleep in the front room. In her free time she likes to play, write and weave baskets.

Seven-year-old Veronica has been part of the programme at Amai for two years. She's in Year Two at School where her favourite lesson is Portuguese. She shares her house with her mother, uncle, sister and older brother. She can't remember her father; he died when she was very young. In her free time she enjoys making baskets and learning embroidery. When she is older she wants to be a cook.

Massoura's father has married twice but lost both his wives. Massoura is in Year Three at school and loves science and maths. When he grows up he wants to be a basket weaver. This is one of his favourite hobbies, along with drawing, playing ball and running.

Seven-year-old Vania is incredibly nervous and hardly ever talks, even to her friends. This is probably related to the death of her parents. She is in Year One at school and likes drawing, basket weaving and playing.

Eight-year-old França lives

nearby in Goto with her mother, two brothers and two sisters. Her father died when she was very young. Franca helps her mother sell fruit, vegetables and charcoal from a table outside their house. She also helps out at home by washing the dishes and lighting the fire. Her favourite lessons are natural sciences, Portuguese and maths.

Jorge, 11, is in Year Three at school where his

favourite subject is maths. In his free time he likes to study, go running, learn embroidery and play football. He has been been going to Amai for two years now, as have his five brothers and sisters. He lives with his mother, uncle and siblings and he wants to be a teacher when he is older.

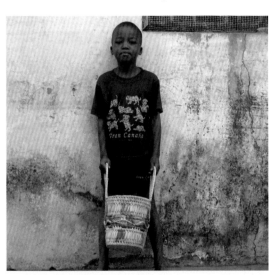

Jose, eight, lost his father to a long illness when

he was young; he wants to be a nurse when he grows up. He lives with his mother and two brothers. He is in his second year at school and likes playing and running.

Ten-year-old Amélia has lost both

parents and lives with her grandmother in the Goto bairro. She is in Year Three at school and has been attending Amai for a year. She likes drawing, weaving and studying. When she grows up she would like to be a nurse.

ACAMO

Blind people face particular difficulties in Beira; there are very few services for them and it's almost impossible for them to find any sort of work, so most are forced to rely on begging for income.

In 2006 ACAMO – the Blind Association of Mozambique – asked BLB for help in funding a small project to train several blind women to do foot and back massages. The project has enabled them to earn some much-needed income from their massage work.

BLB volunteer Claire Bertaud, a Portuguese language student studying at Bristol University who went to Beira in 2009, helped further by producing a poster advertising their services and also by giving some basic English lessons to help them communicate better with foreign clients.

Claire also took part in a day of activities for children with blind mothers. Life is very tough for most of these children; they are not only responsible for looking after their blind parent but often must also help them while they are begging. As a result many don't attend school and end up further marginalised.

The day brought together 14 children who took part in activities such as drawing, writing, races and playing. Their mothers were able to meet other blind women and share their experiences on a range of issues, from the problems of daily life to family planning and HIV/AIDS. It was a much-needed carefree day for both children and mothers – and a rare opportunity for them to meet other people who share their difficulties.

The event was mainly funded by a small individual donation but BLB also contributed to buy some exercise books for the children and a small amount of materials.

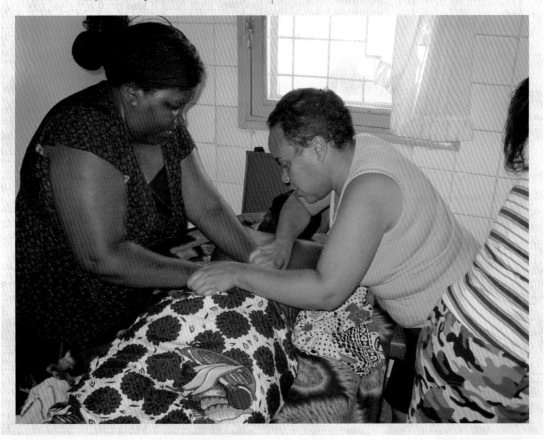

EDUCATION

"Engaging with a school in another part of the world can bring many concepts to life in a very real sense. But it can also do much more than that: it can enable students to reflect on 'difference' and begin to challenge the prejudices and stereotypes that we all grow up with"

Ted Cantle, Institute of Community Cohesion, 2009

BUILDING SCHOOL PARTNERSHIPS

BLB's schools linking programme has been one of the most important and successful aspects of its work in the last two decades.

The first Bristol schools to link up with Beira schools were Portway Community School in Shirehampton; St Thomas Moore in Horfield; and Luckwell Primary in Bedminster. They were followed by Colston's Primary in Cotham; Clifton High School in Clifton; St Bernadette's Primary in Whitchurch.

Luckwell Primary School, which is partnered with Escola Primaria de Matacuane, says the link has played a big part in the school, says deputy head Laura Shore: "The link is as much a part of the structure and ethos of the school as the curriculum, staff and pupils. It would be difficult to imagine a Luckwell not linked with 'the school in Mozambique'."

It's definitely helped to make pupils more aware of diversity, as the school inspection body OFSTED observed when it visited Luckwell in January 2009. It was particularly impressed by the school's efforts to make pupils aware of life outside Bristol, and said: "Pupils display a growing understanding of the diversity of cultures in both Britain and the wider world."

The schools have shared teaching materials and developed joint curriculum programmes for subjects such as the arts, geography, the humanities and English. Sometimes the Bristol schools have raised funds to help their partner schools – enabling them to buy equipment such as a sewing machine or computer, for example.

When Clifton High School donated some money to its link school, the First of May Infant School, teacher Beth Osborne was able to see how they'd spent it when she visited in 2008 with five other teachers.

"The school had spent money on waterproof mattress covers as all the children sleep for two hours every lunchtime" she said. "New tables and chairs for the dining room had also been commissioned by the school and we were able to visit the carpenter at his workshop."

'HUGE BENEFITS FROM THIS TWINNING'

Exchange visits have been key to strengthening the partnerships. To date, almost 20 Bristol teachers have visited Beira (funding their own trips) and a dozen Beira teachers have visited Bristol.

After the Clifton High School teachers' visit of 2008, the school raised funds to bring two teachers from First of May Infant School to Bristol

First of May preschool children learned how to make playdough with Clifton High School teachers.

in 2011. Speaking after their visit, Clifton High lower school head teacher Antony Richards said: "We have had huge benefits from this twinning.

"One example is the phenomenal use the May 1st School makes of recycling – it is their lifeblood, and we have tried to learn from them; it has certainly re-energised our own recycling commitments.

"Their passion for music has had an important influence on our curriculum where the children have played on traditional Mozambican

instruments, and it is not unknown for the aroma of Mozambican rice to be wafting down our corridors, cooked in a traditional oven, a gift from the school.

"To open children's eyes to this fascinating and beautiful culture is something we treasure."

A LIFE-CHANGING EXPERIENCE

For many Bristol teachers, the 5,665-mile trip to Beira has been an emotional, experience – at once inspiring and shocking.

Jill Ritchie has twice visited Beira as international education officer with Bristol City Council, the first of which was with a delegation of head teachers in 1999.

She recalls how dilapidated the buildings were: "You could see the evidence of war everywhere. People were camping in these dilapidated buildings but there were no services like water or electricity."

Despite being shocked at the poverty they witnessed, the trip was "fantastic, a life-changing experience", says Jill. "It really made us think more deeply about our values and what was important in life, and what education was really for. It was also a real master class in leadership."

The Bristol teachers came back armed with masses of material to use in joint curriculum projects, on topics ranging from sustainability and use of resources to geography. "For example, a simple question such as 'how do you get to school?' can open up a lot of discussion because Mozambican children might walk a long way," she explains.

Above all, the Bristol teachers were reminded of the fact that children are essentially the same the world over. Jill recalls a project in which children were given disposable cameras and asked to photograph the things that were important to them.

She says: "They were exactly the sort of things any child would photograph – their bicycle, their brother or sister, playing games."

EDUCATION OVERVIEW

Because the Portuguese did not invest in education in its colonies, Mozambique was estimated to have a literacy rate of only 10% when it gained independence in 1975. Hardly surprisingly, raising this rate was a priority for the new Frelimo government, which made education compulsory between the ages of six and 12.

The civil war destroyed much of these plans, however, along with at least 50% of primary schools. When the war ended in 1992, the literacy rate was 40% and only 60% of children were in primary school (7% were in secondary school).

The education system is slowly being rebuilt but the destruction of school buildings and lack of qualified teachers has made this is an uphill task.

However, as the former Mozambican High Commissioner to Britain, Antonio Gumende highlighted in a speech in Bristol, Mozambique has made great strides. The number of school children in the education system has increased from 2.3 million in 2000 to over 5 million in 2009.

Approximately around 81% of Mozambique's six to 12-year-olds now attend primary school, although far fewer – 20% – attend secondary school.

Education is compulsory for seven years but students may miss years of schooling because they've not passed their end-of-year exams or because the school doesn't have room for them or, if they're secondary students, because they can't afford to study that year.

The literacy rate is 55% for men and 41% for women.

Mozambique now has one of the highest economic growth rates in the world – it was over 8% in 2011. In fact, of the ten countries in the world which had the highest growth rates in the last decade, six were in Africa.

The Mozambican government is now engaged in the process of opening up coal mines, gas fields and oil fields, with the help of partners from abroad. The government hopes to use some of their new-found wealth, when it is properly established, to improve education (and other public services).

A COMMON GOAL

Emma Drew of Luckwell Primary School concluded that teachers are the same the world over after her visit to Beira in 2002.

Describing their Beira welcome as "extremely warm, almost overwhelming", she said there was "tremendous enthusiasm for our work and we enjoyed working alongside the Beira teachers and learning from each other".

She added: "The experience clearly illustrated the many similarities between teachers across the world. All the teachers concerned want the very best for their children and we felt that a curriculum that values the inclusion of global concerns and understanding is our common goal."

SPARKING A RIOT...

Two decades after Jill Ritchie's first visit, Bristol teachers are still shocked by the conditions in which their Beira colleagues work – and impressed by their commitment.

When nine teachers from Colston's Primary School, Portway School, Luckwell Primary School, and St Bernadette's Primary & Junior School visited their sister schools in Beira in 2009, they described the state of some of the schools as "a health and safety nightmare, with broken windows and crumbling concrete".

But they were amazed at how well behaved the pupils were and impressed by the Beira teachers' commitment in dealing with more than 80 students in a class, says Bristol International Twinnings co-ordinator Alix Hughes who went with them.

Not everything went to plan, however. Some of the Bristol teachers had created a football-based activity for a class of 25 primary school pupils which would work perfectly well somewhere like Whitchurch, recalls Alix. "But in a school of more than 4,000 pupils, it actually caused a riot with some children being forced back into their classrooms amidst clouds of dust and sand."

'NOT ALONE ON THIS PLANET'

Mozambican musician and storyteller Celso Paco, who visits Bristol every autumn to run workshops and assemblies in schools here, is a huge fan of the schools' linking programme. He recalls how important it was to him as a boy to learn about other cultures and says Beira children can only benefit from making contact with other children on the other side of the world, in the same age group.

"They learn that there are children with other ways of living that are different from their own, but with the same aim of becoming somebody in the future," he says.

Although teaching conditions are different in Beira with as many as 80 pupils in a class, there are also many similarities with Bristol schools.

"And they learn the importance of help. As their schools were destroyed during the civil war, the children of Bristol have provided them with materials such as pencils, toys, exercise books and so on. In this way, they experience the sense of not being alone on this planet."

Teresa Muandionessa Tirivangama, head of Matecuane primary, and Matias Traquino Afonso Junior, head of English at Macuti primary, visit the museum to see the twin town's batik banners.

THIS CLOSENESS AND FRIENDSHIP

BLB volunteer Joe Budge visited Amina Sebastao, head of Escola Primeiro de Mayo Primary (First of May Infant School), which is twinned with Clifton High School, in March 2012 to ask her what she thought of BLB's school partnership programme.

JOE: "What are the benefits to your link with Bristol?"

AMINA: "The experience and the exchanging of experience, beyond just the travel. Through the friendship we have gained more experiences and learnt other activities which we use with our pre-school pupils.

"Also through games, furniture and other material, for example, we have this computer [one of two in her office] and other equipment as a result of the link and also the paint to paint the school.

"But beyond the material things, we have also benefited from the human contact and the things and games we have learnt, for example Play-doh and Plasticine. Play-doh itself is too expensive for us to buy but we learnt to make it using flour and other cheaper materials, thanks to the friendship."

JOE: "How has the Link helped the students educationally or culturally?"

AMINA: "We have lots of materials from England, lots of books written in English and lots of pictures. We show the children the pictures and teach them about the culture of the pupils on the other side of the world and how they play."

JOE: "What do you like most about the link with Bristol?"

AMINA: "This closeness and friendship; the material things are good but it's the communication between us which has been important. It's the contact between people. Our trip to England [in 2011] was great and now we are trying to implement the things we saw there in Bristol and it is all very useful and important for our school."

JOE: "What are your hopes for the future for the link with BLB?"

AMINA: "I hope to strengthen the link, I hope the communication gets stronger because the friendship already exists."

CULTURE

"You cannot dance well on only one leg"
Mozambican proverb

THE POWER OF ART AND MUSIC

Cultural exchange is one of Bristol Link with Beira's most successful and important activities and is seen as a core way to increase understanding and fellowship between Bristol and Beira. To that end, BLB has brought storytellers and filmmakers, artists and union leaders, teachers and politicians to Bristol.

MUSIC

Some of BLB's most successful cultural exchanges have involved Mozambican musicians. Visitors to Mozambique often comment on how important music is in the country; it's a key feature of Mozambican life and is even used in schools on a regular basis.

The first Mozambican band to play in Bristol was Mabulu (whose name means 'looking for a dialogue') at Bristol's Fiddlers Club in July 2002. Mabulu featured two of the respected "grand old men" of Mozambiquan music, *marrabenta* musicians Dilon Djindi and Lisboa Matavel, as well as Mozambican rapper Chiquito from Mad Level, nominated for the newcomer award in BBC Radio 3's World Music Awards.

Marrabenta is a form of Mozambican dance music that originated in the 1930s and 1940s and merges traditional Mozambican rhythms, Portuguese folk and Western pop.

The following year, young Beira musicians, including the group Djaaka, played in several Bristol schools, singing songs of slavery and leading drum and dance sessions with pupils that were described as "quite phenomenal".

Their songs tackle contemporary issues such as AIDS, poverty and social division – difficult subjects delivered through an urgent and infectious beat. As one reviewer said: 'The warm and fluid Djaaka sound makes itself irresistible to all those within earshot who fancy giving their limbs a little workout."

The Beira band Mussodji was one of the star

Beira musicians Mussodji playing on the Colston Hall Stage at the Harbour Festival. (Pic: Mark Simmons)

Mussodji hunt and kill wild animals to make their clothes and instruments.

bands at the Bristol Harbour Festival in 2007 as part of Abolition 200, a year of events to mark the 200th anniversary of the abolition of the slave trade. Its performance also marked Beira's 100th birthday.

FILMS

BLB has both arranged for Mozambican films to be screened in Bristol and also made a short film itself. The film it commissioned was a 20-minute film documentary prepared for use during International Women's Day 2009 in Bristol.

It featured the Director of the Department for Women and Social Services, women from some of the organisations that BLB helps (ACAMO, ACRIDEME and Amai Mussananhi) and women from one of the local markets.

"Making the film was an enjoyable, if slightly stressful at times, experience and we understand that the film was a useful, popular and moving addition to the IWD programme and is continuing to be used," said BITA coordinator Alix Hughes.

In 2007 Mozambican High Commissioner, His Excellency Antonio Gumende visited Bristol for one of BLB's fundraising 'Meals for Mozambique', during which the film *Marranbentando – The Stories My Guitar Sings* was shown. It was the first time the film – which features the music of Mozambique – had been shown in the UK.

That same year, BLB worked with the Afrika Eye festival to bring the Mozambican film director, Gabriel Mondlane, to Bristol to talk about and show a series of his films. His visit included a lecture at the University of the West of England.

STORIES

Storytelling is another traditional art form. Mozambican culture is rich in tales, proverbs, myths, and jokes that have been passed down from generation to generation. Storyteller and musician Celso Paco has introduced hundreds of Bristol schoolchildren to this tradition though his annual visits to schools here since 2004. See Celso Paco section on page 67.

EXHIBITIONS

In 2010, BLB volunteer and keen snapper Claire Bertaud created an exhibition of her photographs of Beira in the Department of Hispanic, Portuguese and Latin American Studies at the University of Bristol. It proved so popular that it is still on view there – where it is inspiring new generations of students studying Portuguese to spend some time volunteering for BLB in Beira.

THRONE OF WEAPONS

"The purpose of the project is to disarm the minds of people and to disarm the hands of people"

Bishop Dinis Sengulane, 2005

The Throne of Weapons was made by Mozambican artist Cristóvão Estevão Canhavato, better known as Kester, in 2001 from sawn-up AK47s and other guns left over from the recent war.

This eloquent testimony to both the suffering of Mozambique's past and the hope of its future was the result of an extraordinary programme devised by an Anglican priest, Dinis Sengulane, Bishop of Libombos.

The Bishop had spent a sleepless night following a conference on peace and reconciliation because he knew Mozambique's peace was threatened by the presence of millions of weapons left in the country after the war.

Taking his inspiration from the Bible – specifically Isaiah's prophecy, "They shall beat their swords into ploughshares, and their spears into pruning hooks", he began a programme called 'Transforming Arms into Tools'.

Run by the Christian Council of Mozambique and supported by Christian Aid, the programme enabled people to swap weapons for 'instruments of production' such as sewing machines, ploughs and bicycles. Children could hand in unused bullets for school pens and exercise books, and when a group of farmers found a cache of 500 guns, they exchanged

Mozambican artists and sculptors making a large tree of life from weapons which now stands in the British Museum courtyard."

them for a tractor. More than 600,000 weapons were exchanged and destroyed in this way.

In 2002, the Throne was bought by the British Museum and in 2005 it went on tour around the country. BLB worked with Bristol Museum and Art Gallery to make sure the Throne came to Bristol.

It spent a month here and BLB organised a series of educational and cultural activities, including music, food, craft, dance and visits to two schools, to accompany it. The Throne had a huge impact, prompting all kinds of debate ranging from local gun crime and conflict resolution to the transforming power of art and sustainable development.

The Throne is on permanent display in the British Museum's Sainsbury African Galleries in London.

STORYTELLER AND MUSICIAN CELSO PACO

Traditional Mozambican musician and storyteller Celso Paco has been visiting Bristol every autumn to run workshops and assemblies in schools since 1994. He's also led story-telling sessions in Bristol Central Library. Celso's visits are one of the most popular activities organised by BLB – and Celso enjoys it almost as much as the schoolchildren.

"To share cultural experiences with the children is very rewarding and enriching and to recognise one another on each visit is a treasure for both sides," he says. "I enjoy the fact that I can help my fellow Mozambicans to spread our culture, which has been suppressed under colonial time. As a child, I was fortunate to learn about other cultures when international groups visited my school in Mozambique. Now is my turn to pay back."

Maputo-born Celso is a percussionist who has played all over the world with jazz musicians from both the USA and Europe. Now based in Sweden, he incorporates traditional Mozambican stories, which his grandparents told him, in his workshops, building in sounds, dance and movements in traditional Karangana style. Celso also introduces the children to Mozambican instruments, such as the *marimba* (a type of xylophone), *ngoma* (drum), *xitende* (bow) and *mbira* (thumb piano).

He is enormously popular with the youngsters of Easton Church of England primary school and Luckwell primary school in Bedminster, as well as with older pupils at Clifton High School. The children love learning Mozambican dances and songs, and listening to Celso's stories about Mozambican history and culture, says Belinda Wallace, a teacher at Colston's Primary, Cotham.

Speaking after his 2010 visit, Belinda said: "We had a fantastic two days with Celso. All the classes had a session with him and I've had lots of good feedback. As Portuguese was our language of the term, the children were also able to greet and thank him in Portuguese."

Celso loves the workshops: "The response from the children is always good, especially when I teach them songs and dances. They show respect, pay attention and enjoy being active during my interactive story-telling."

And he is clear about the benefits to Bristol schoolchildren: "It is good to learn about other people's culture. And the best way is to have someone visiting from a given country.

"Children in Bristol become motivated to know about their own culture when they have someone else sharing his or her own. They learn to be proud of who they are and to respect others, regardless of where they come from," he says.

Celso's sister, Lucrecia Paco is Mozambique's most famous actress, has also performed her one-woman show in schools and Bristol museum here.

* Celso has released a CD, Dugong, recorded with the Sweden-based band Dynamo Deluxe. His music is influenced by the dance and music scene in Mozambique's capital, Maputo, where he was born, but he is also inspired by the music of neighbouring Zimbabwe and South Africa.

QUESTIONS, QUESTIONS...

Bristol schoolchildren are always intrigued by Celso's workshops and endlessly curious about him and his culture – so what kind of information do they want from him? Celso says the most frequent questions are:

- Do children in Beira have pets?
- Can all children in Mozambique go to school?
- What kind of food is there in Mozambique?
- Do you have children?
- How did you learn to play all your instruments?
- What is your favourite instrument among them?
- Are these true stories?
- How old are you?

A TYPICAL CELSO WORKSHOP

The workshop usually starts with students clapping to a beat and saying their names and welcoming each other. Then Celso introduces them to a variety of traditional musical instruments, playing them first before giving students a chance to try them out themselves. He tells them two or three stories and at the end everyone discusses the moral of each one. One story might relate to selfish behaviour by a villager during the great Mozambican floods of 2000; another might discuss the polluting of a village well. Celso's story-telling always involves movement and dance, which the students take part in, wearing *capulanas*, a traditional brightly coloured cloth worn in Mozambique, which is wrapped around the body and tied loosely.

LIFE

"If you have no teeth, do not break the clay cooking pot"
Mozambican proverb

MOZAMBICAN FOOD

A strong Portuguese influence runs throughout Mozambican cuisine where dishes such as the fiery hot piri piri chicken sit alongside traditional African recipes such as *matapa*, a seafood stew (clam, crab or prawn) made with cassava leaves and served over rice. Beira's position on the coast means fish and seafood are also a vital part of the cuisine; indeed, Mozambican fish, shellfish, shrimp, and prawns are considered to be among the finest in the world.

You'll find mouth-watering dishes such as *macaza* (grilled shellfish kebabs), *bacalhão* (dried salted cod) and *chocos* (squid cooked in its own ink) on the menu, along with stews flavoured with onions, peppers and coconut.

In rural areas, the two staple crops grown in Mozambique are corn and cassava, both of which were introduced from the Americas by the Portuguese. The cassava root – 'mandioca' in Portuguese – is so important that its name means "the all-sufficient". It can be baked, dried in the sun, mashed with water to form a kind of porridge or ground into coarse flour. Other staples include corn flour porridge (*massa*), rice and beans.

Alcoholic drinks include locally distilled *sura* (palm wine), *ntondondo* (cashew fruit spirit) and *nipa* (sugarcane spirit) while *aguardente* (brandy) and *vinho tinto e branca* (red and white wine) are imported from Portugal and South Africa. Mozambique's breweries produce excellent *cerveja* (beer).

Celebrating Mozambican food through its regular 'Meal for Mozambique' events has been one of BLB's most regular fund-raising activities. This was the menu for the 2008 Meal for Mozambique:

- **SWEET PEA SOUP:** made from sweet potatoes and peas, a traditional soup in Mozambique
- **ROAST CHICKEN THIGHS AND PIRI PIRI SAUCE:** this hot and spicy condiment illustrates the influence and symbiosis of Mozambican and Portuguese cooking
- **BEEF STEW:** meat stew is the staple of many African cuisines, served along with yam, maize, rize or potato
- **CURRIED POTATOES:** inspired by a Ugandan recipe
- **CURRIED CARROTS:** inspired by a Tanzanian recipe with mustard, tumeric and lemons
- **TABOULLEH:** salad made of bulgar wheat, shallots, tomatoes and lemon vinaigrette and mint – North African cuisine

MOZAMBICAN RECIPES

Want to cook your own Mozambican meal? Why not try one of these traditional recipes.

MATATA (CLAM AND PEANUT SOUP)

Serve 6

INGREDIENTS

1 cup onions, chopped finely;

2 oz olive oil;

4 cups chopped clams or other fish;

1 cup peanuts chopped finely;

2 tomatoes cut into small pieces;

1 tbsp salt;

½ tsp black pepper;

1 tsp cayenne pepper crushed;

1½ cups of fresh spinach chopped finely;

2 cups white rice

Matata is a typical Mozambican entrée, made with pumpkin leaves and is not influenced by Portuguese cooking. Imagine a combination of clams and peanuts and tender young greens. You may want to start without the crushed pepper, adding it gradually and discretely.

Sauté onions in olive oil until soft but not brown. Add clams, peanuts, tomatoes, salt, black pepper and cayenne pepper. Simmer gently for 30 mins. Add spinach and cover tightly. As soon as the leaves have wilted, it's ready to serve. Cook rice in 5 ups of boiling water until tender.

SQUASH SOUP

Serve 6 as a first course or 4 as a light meal

INGREDIENTS

1-2 1bs squash, peeled and cubed;

4-5 large garlic cloves crushed;

1 tbsp oil or butter;

1 tsp black pepper';

¼ tsp curry powder;

1-3 tbsp lemon juice;

bay leaf;

1 tbsp onion minced;

1 tsp salt;

1 tsp fresh ginger grated;

1 tsp paprika

Boil squash in just enough water to cover. When pieces are very soft, lift out, leaving water in the pan, and mash with a fork or put through a sieve. Return to cooking water; add bay leaf and simmer gently.

Meanwhile, sautée the crushed garlic and onion in the oil or butter. Combine remaining spices and add to the butter mixture. Sauté over a low heat for 5-10 minutes until the flavours are well blended, then spoon a little of the squash liquid into the butter mixture and stir. Pour entire mixture into the soup pan. Add water to make about 6 cups, and stir in lemon juice to taste (chicken stock may be used instead of water).

THE MARVELOUS CAPULANA

"A real Mozambican woman must have a capulana. Two capulanas. A thousand capulanas or more – the number doesn't matter... There can never be too many"
– Paulina Chiziane

Mozambican women will tell you there is no garment as versatile and useful as the *capulana*, the length of waxed cotton cloth which they wear in all sorts of ways – wrapped around the waist as a skirt, used as an extra wrap when the temperature drops, slung over the shoulder as a baby carrier or even worn as a headdress.

So important is the *capulana* that the Mozambican writer Paulina Chiziane describes it as "the symbol of Mozambican women, of African women".

She adds: "A real Mozambican woman must have a *capulana*. Two *capulanas*. A thousand capulanas or more – the number doesn't matter. One *capulana* is never the same as another. There can never be too many."

Typically measuring two metres by one metre, the ever-practical *capulana* can also function as an instant towel, an extra bed covering or a door curtain; they can even be used as a makeshift bundle to carry a baby, grains or beans. They are cool in hot temperatures, easy to pack and carry and don't need sewing.

In fact, so deeply ingrained in Mozambican culture are capulanas that a woman who bears herself well in times of difficulty is said to "tie her *capulana* well". The former Prime Minister Luisa Diogo is described as a woman with a firm *capulana*, a phrase that encapsulates her power and dignity.

As Paulina says: "The *capulana* does not age, but is eternally renewed. It is the best cloth in the world."

The traditional and versatile capulana is an important symbol of Mozambican women and can be found for sale at market stalls throughout the country.

BRISTOL LINK WITH BEIRA: THE NEXT 20 YEARS

BLB Secretary Dave Spurgeon has been involved with Bristol Link with Beira since its early days. He assesses the last two decades and looks ahead to the next 20 years

In looking forward to try and predict how BLB will develop over the next 20 years – or even 20 months – it's instructive to look back to remind ourselves of the purpose of the link. It's a twinning that was always intended to be of benefit to both communities, and to a large extent BLB has delivered on that aim.

We have listened to what the people of Beira have identified as priorities; that has resulted in the development of the projects identified in this publication. Mozambique is a very different place than when the Friendship Agreement was signed in 1990. The 1992 Peace Accord has brought stability to the country and there has been sustained and considerable economic growth over the past few years. That brings opportunities. In Bristol the Link is well established and respected, especially within the schools linked with Beira and our partner organisations.

There is an energy boom in Mozambique, with coal, gas and oil deposits being developed. Although companies in Bristol may not be able to help with the initial developments, there will be big supply chains that we could get involved with, in partnership with local companies. This could increase links between our two cities, as we see Mozambique's economy develop rapidly in the next 20 years. However, despite its economic growth, Mozambique remains a poor country and the twinning is still unequal – of more benefit to Beira than Bristol. The current global downturn,

which disproportionally affects Southern Africa, is unlikely to reverse that situation in the short term. It also means that it will be harder to fundraise in Bristol both from individuals and institutions.

Equally, Southern Africa is a not a region of the world that currently attracts much attention here and, when it does, the focus is on South Africa. Bristol's link with Beira remains the only civic link that Britain has with Mozambique.

Finally, Mozambique does not have a strong civil society or voluntary and community sector, and relatively few 'home grown' sustainable NGOs, thus reducing the capacity to develop projects with local people on the ground.

While these challenges continue to outweigh the opportunities, maintaining the link will continue to be a challenge. However, the current Trustees remain committed to try and address a number of these issues. We are working with our partners in Mozambique to establish a sister NGO in Beira, serviced and run by local Mozambicans, to create ownership and visibility. This would potentially open both organisations to greater funding and development opportunities.

We will continue to develop new projects while attempting to make existing ones more sustainable through open dialogue with our partners here and civil society and local government in Beira. These are uncertain but exciting times. We look forward to reporting even greater success in another 20 years.

MOZAMBIQUE TIMELINE

EARLY YEARS

STONE AGE: The first people to live in the area are San hunters and gatherers, descendents of Africa's earliest peoples.

1ST TO 5TH CENTURIES AD: Bantu-speaking peoples migrate from northern and western Africa. The Bantu are farmers, cattle herders and ironworkers. They use iron to make weapons to conquer their neighbours.

5TH CENTURY ONWARDS: Arab, Persian and Asian traders start trading with Bantu clans living along the coast, exchanging African gold, ivory, shells and skins for silks and spices from Asia and India. Arab seafarers make Mozambique part of an extensive trading system linking Africa's entire east coast with Arabia and India. Arab traders settle in the region and create a mixed Islamic-African culture that becomes known as Swahili.

1000 ONWARDS: Bantu kingdoms and empires expand all over East Africa. Mozambique is home to numerous kingdoms, including a Shona empire called Mutapa, which possesses rich goldmines, later believed by Europeans to be the legendary mines of King Solomon. By the 14th century, many of the coastal trading towns have become independent city-states.

1498: Portuguese explorer Vasco da Gama visits the area during his voyage searching for a sea route to the East. He finds a sophisticated trading society with a monetary economy, wealthy merchants and ships whose navigational charts and instruments are better than his. This is a fractious first visit (da Gama's paltry gifts are scorned by the ruling Sultan and he leaves in a hurry, firing his canons at the hostile crowd). However, it marks the next stage in Mozambique's history: the arrival of the Europeans.

PORTUGUESE RULE

1500 ONWARDS: Portugal seizes the area as part of its territorial expansion into East Africa, calling it Terra da Boa Gente ('Country of the Good People') and destroying much of the existing African-Islamic civilisation in their conquest. Portugal's interest is trade but it is also motivated by the desire to promote Christianity and suppress Islam. However, its influence spreads only gradually because its attention is mainly focussed on its activities in India and Brazil. Individual settlers and officials enjoy a great deal of autonomy and power, and African kingdoms such as the Mwene Matapa and Swahili merchants still dominate the area.

1600s: The Portuguese explore further into the continent, subduing the inhabitants, taking control of gold mines and encouraging Portuguese farmers – many of them ex-felons and former soldiers – to settle in the region. A Portuguese man can seize whatever land he wants and use its people for labour, enjoying total control over their lives, provided he pays the 'Prazo' tax to the Portuguese crown.

1700s-1800s: Portugal faces constant challenges on two sides: African tribes reluctant to accept Portuguese rule and the settlers ('prazeiros') who increasingly rebel against paying taxes to Portugal. The slave trade, which has always existed here, expands rapidly, exporting the healthiest, youngest and strongest members of the population to misery, and becomes Mozambique's most important business. Conflicts break out between different Bantu tribes; some profit by being slave traders themselves while others are hunted to extinction. One million slaves are shipped from Mozambique during the 1800s. The slave trade is abolished in 1878 only after missionary-explorer David Livingstone publishes a report on conditions in Mozambique.

1885 ONWARDS: At a conference in Berlin, European countries agree to divide Africa between them. Portugal claims Mozambique but can only control the south, leasing out large parts to private trading companies, which enjoy enormous power.

LATE 1800s: There is a constant resistance to Portuguese rule. The powerful Gaza empire in the south is one of the most active Bantu tribes in rebelling against the Portuguese until its ruler is captured, transported to Portugal and paraded through the streets.

EARLY 1900s: After the fall of the Gaza empire, Portugal finally has full control of Mozambique. Large parts are still leased to private companies which own all rights to agriculture and mining in their area. The companies use forced labour ('chibalo') in their plantations and mines, with flogging a regular form of punishment. The companies also supply cheap, often forced, labour elsewhere, including South Africa's Transvaal gold mines. Conditions are so bad in Mozambique that many people flee to neighbouring British colonies.

1917: Mozambique's first major anti-colonial uprising of the 20th century was a Shona rebellion which saw Portuguese military bases overrun. It took three years for the authorities to restore order in Mozambique.

1930s: Portugal, which has been in the grip of a fascist military dictatorship since 1926, encourages migration to Mozambique and the population grows rapidly. But Portugal is not interested in developing Mozambique or its people; schools and hospitals are for the use of Portuguese citizens only and Africans are banned by law from setting up in business. The illiteracy rate is over 90% and Mozambicans can avoid forced labour only if they give up their culture and beliefs, and become "assimilados". As part of the deal, they must wear shoes, eat with a knife and fork and prove they don't sleep on the floor. Only 1% become assimilados.

"The Portuguese stand out [in the colonial debate] because they boasted the most and did the least. After close to half a thousand years, not a single medical doctor had been trained in Portuguese Mozambique" **Guyanese historian Walter Rodney**

1940s-1950s: After World War II, European countries begin to grant independence to their colonies but Portugal stubbornly refuses. In Mozambique, the colonial government enforces an oppressive, racist regime; Africans have to carry a book to be signed every day by their employers. So restrictive are its rules that by 1950, only 4,353 Mozambicans out of 5.7 million have been granted the right to vote.

Communist and anti-colonial ideologies spread throughout Africa and clandestine Mozambique independence movements develop but Portugal swiftly crushes any overt signs of independence. African farmers who form business co-operatives are swiftly jailed. Dissatisfaction flares up in riots and strikes, which are brutally suppressed with beatings and sometimes deaths.

JUNE 16, 1960: Hundreds of people are killed by Government troops in a peaceful demonstration in Mueda. The Mueda Massacre only inflames the demand for independence.

1961: 'Chibalo' – forced labour – is finally abolished.

1962: The Frente de Libertação de Moçambique (Frelimo, also known as the Front for the Liberation of Mozambique) is formed in neighbouring Tanzania with the aim of overthrowing Portuguese rule. It begins an armed guerrilla campaign in 1964. Within two years most provinces in Northern Mozambique are under Frelimo control; within three years one seventh of the population and one fifth of the territory are in Frelimo hands.

The Portuguese find it difficult to counter Frelimo's hit-and-run tactics, particularly in rural areas where the guerrillas melt away into the bush. Later Frelimo uses landmines to devastating effect both on Portuguese lives and morale, causing a paralysing 'mine psychosis' among Portuguese troops who fear stepping on a landmine. But the tactic also has a devastating impact on civilians who still suffer from the legacy of landmines today.

1969: Frelimo president Eduardo Mondlane is killed by a letter bomb in Tanzania; the Portuguese secret service is blamed. At his funeral, Mondlane is described as having "laid down his life for the truth that man was made for dignity and self-determination". Frelimo's 7,000-strong guerrillas continue the fight against Portugal's 70,000 troops.

INDEPENDENCE AT LAST

1975: The battle for independence is overtaken by events in Portugal when the fascist regime is overturned by a leftist military coup in 1974. This brings about a dramatic change in Portuguese policy and on June 25, 1975, Portugal hands over power to Frelimo.

MUEDA MASSACRE

In his book, *The Struggle for Mozambique*, published in 1969, Eduardo Mondlane, first leader of Mozambique's liberation movement Frelimo, quotes this account of the Mueda Massacre from Alburto-Joaquim Chipande, then aged 22.

"The Portuguese sent police through the villages inviting people to a meeting at Mueda. Several thousand people came to hear what the Portuguese would say... Then the governor invited our leaders into the administrator's office. I was waiting outside. They were in there for four hours.

"When they came out on the verandah, the governor asked the crowd who wanted to speak. Many wanted to speak, and the governor told them all to stand on one side. Then without another word he ordered the police to bind the hands of those who had stood on one side, and the police began beating them. I was close by. I saw it all.

"When the people saw what was happening, they began to demonstrate against the Portuguese, and the Portuguese simply ordered the police trucks to come and collect these arrested persons. So there were more demonstrations against this.

"At that moment the troops were still hidden, and the people went up close to the police to stop the arrested persons from being taken away. So the governor called the troops, and when they appeared he told them to open fire. They killed about 600 people... I myself escaped because I was close to a graveyard where I could take cover, and then I ran away."

Mozambique is at last an independent nation, the People's Republic of Mozambique, with Samora Machel as the first president, but it is in a desperate state. Portugal pulls out rapidly, as do around 300,000 white settlers, including virtually all the skilled professionals. As they retreat, they destroy as much as they can – houses, livestock, cars, infrastructure, machinery.

The new, inexperienced Frelimo-based Government is left with a country that is in a state of chaos and economic collapse, with almost no resources and a population that has not been educated. It starts to form a radical new society along Marxist-Leninist principles, establishing local committees to restart industry and farming, taking over land and houses, making private hospitals and schools public, nationalising banks and companies and giving priority to education.

Frelimo's initial attempts to overturn traditional hierarchies, such as local chiefs, and send thousands of dissidents to 're-education camps' alienate people and lead to internal tensions.

1977-1992: But much worse is to come: a new guerrilla movement, the Mozambique National Resistance Movement (Renamo), established and funded by Rhodesia (now Zimbabwe) and later South Africa, begins a bloody civil war against Frelimo. It will rage from 1977 to 1992 and claim over a million lives in fighting and starvation. It will also set back Mozambique's development by decades.

1992: Frelimo and Renamo sign a peace accord, bringing peace to Mozambique at last.

LINKS WITH OTHER ORGANISATIONS

Bristol International Twinning Association
www.bristol.gov.uk/page/twinning
www.bristolbeiralink.org
BITA is an umbrella organisation that provides direct support to Bristol's seven individual twinning associations – with Beira, Bordeaux, Guangzhou, Hannover, Oporto, Puerto Morazan and Tblisi. It supports civic and cultural exchanges and works to develop international development activities such as global education programmes in schools.

ACTSA – Action for Southern Africa
www.actsa.org
A membership organisation working with the people of southern Africa for justice, democracy and development in the region, ACTSA was founded in 1994 as the successor organisation to the Anti-Apartheid Movement (AAM), to develop and promote solidarity in the UK and internationally with southern Africa.

Bristol ACTSA
www.actsabristol.co.uk
Bristol ACTSA was established in March 1995 and works to help build democracy and development across the region. It also fundraises to support a number of projects in Southern Africa. Contact Bristol ACTSA secretary Sheila Roberts on sheilamaryroberts@btinternet.com or 0117 9719912.

Beira Chamber of Commerce (Associação de Comércio e Indãstria)
www.acismoz.com
An apolitical, autonomous, private, non-profit association founded in 2000, ACIS promotes commerce and industry in Beira. It has more than 300 members representing a combined investment of US$70 billion.

High Commission of the Republic of Mozambique
www.mozambiquehighcommission.org.uk
The face of Mozambique in the UK, the High Commission is headed by His Excellency Mr Carlos dos Santos.

Bristol City Council
www.bristol.gov.uk
The gateway to information and services about Bristol City Council.

Young Africa
http://youngafrica.org
Young Africa empowers young people through practical skills training and by encouraging them to earn a decent living through income-generating projects. It teaches them skills of hands – to make them self-reliant; skills of heart and mind – to live with dignity and responsibility; and skills of the soul – to live with purpose.

Motivation UK
www.motivation.org.uk
Motivation is an international development charity supporting people with mobility disabilities. Its high-quality, low-cost wheelchairs are designed specifically for use in poor countries.

Brandon Trust
www.brandontrust.org
Brandon Trust is a Bristol-based UK charity working throughout the South West of England, employing nearly 2000 people who support approximately 1500 people with learning disabilities to live the lives they choose.

Coaching for Hope
www.coachingforhope.org
Coaching for Hope taps into the global passion for football to create better futures for young people in West and Southern Africa. Professional coaches from the UK train local youth workers to recognised FA standards. At the same time, the local coaches learn how to deliver HIV awareness and life skills sessions to young people in their communities.

Skill share International
www.skillshare.org
Skillshare International is an international volunteering and development organisation that works in partnership with communities in Africa and Asia to reduce poverty, injustice and inequality and to further economic and social development.